THE NEW SCIENCE OF LEARNING

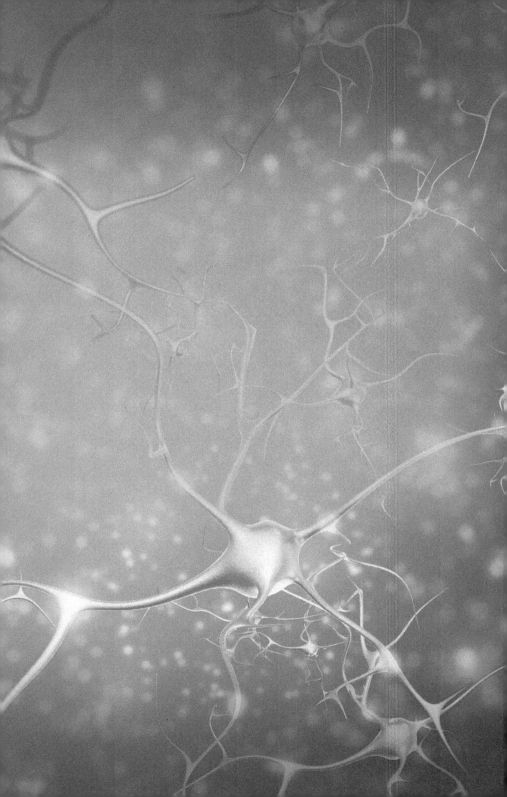

Terry Doyle and
Todd Zakrajsek

THE NEW
SCIENCE of
LEARNING

How to Learn in Harmony
With Your Brain

SECOND EDITION

Foreword by
Kathleen F. Gabriel

STERLING, VIRGINIA

Published by Stylus Publishing, LLC.
22883 Quicksilver Drive
Sterling, Virginia 20166-2019

Library of Congress Cataloging-in-Publication Data
Names: Doyle, Terry, 1951- author. | Zakrajsek, Todd, author.
Title: The new science of learning: how to learn in harmony with your
    brain / Terry Doyle and Todd Zakrajsek.
Description: Second Edition. | Sterling, Virginia: Stylus Publishing, LLC,
    [2018] | Includes bibliographical references and index.
Identifiers: LCCN 2018022978 (print) | LCCN 2018023565 (ebook) |
    ISBN 9781620366592 (ePub. mobi) | ISBN 9781620366585 (uPDF) |
    ISBN 9781620366561 (cloth: acid-free paper) | ISBN 9781620366578
    (paperback: acid-free paper) | ISBN 9781620366585 (library
    networkable e-edition) | ISBN 9781620366592 (consumer e-edition)
Subjects: LCSH: Learning ability. | Learning, Psychology of. | Brain. | Study
    skills.
Classification: LCC LB1134 (ebook) | LCC LB1134.D68 2018 (print) |
    DDC 371.33/4—dc23
LC record available at https://lccn.loc.gov/2018022978

13-digit ISBN: 978-1-62036-656-1 (cloth)
13-digit ISBN: 978-1-62036-657-8 (paperback)
13-digit ISBN: 978-1-62036-658-5 (library networkable e-edition)
13-digit ISBN: 978-1-62036-659-2 (consumer e-edition)

Printed in the United States of America

All first editions printed on acid-free paper
that meets the American National Standards Institute
Z39-48 Standard.

Bulk Purchases
Quantity discounts are available for use in workshops and
for staff development.
Call 1-800-232-0223

First Edition, 2013

To Tallulah Bligh Mekkes,
my granddaughter, the newest lover of
learning in the Doyle family
                    —Terry Doyle

To students who strive to be better learners, for
such efforts hold the potential to benefit us all.
                    —Todd Zakrajsek

CONTENTS

CONTENTS

FOREWORD

The second edition of *The New Science of Learning: How to Learn in Harmony With Your Brain* is a fascinating book for students and a valuable resource for professors, advisers, tutors in academic support centers, and even athletic coaches. Terry Doyle and Todd Zakrajsek have updated their book to include the latest research on how the human brain learns and factors that can help increase learning power by using researched-based strategies. In every-day terms, they break down the *scientific* workings of the brain and give practical advice that students can use to help increase their learning and recall, especially when challenged with difficult tasks.

In today's world, it can be overwhelming to come to grips with the vast amount of course materials and information that college students have to scrutinize every day. Nevertheless, the contents of this book can be beneficial in helping students become efficient and effective learners not only for college but also for their future careers. In chapter 1, "A New Look at Learning," Doyle and Zakrajsek provide vital steps students can take to prepare themselves for learning. They explain why and how sleep, nutrition, hydration, and exercise are vital for getting our brains ready to learn and how our brains experience a change in neurochemistry when we learn new information. The human brain needs energy in order to function at its best. By the end of chapter 1, readers won't be able to put this book down. It is a fascinating read that helps readers recognize that even though new learning can (and dare I say, should) be challenging and difficult, the time and effort put into gaining new knowledge can be optimize and enhanced.

Additionally, each chapter includes specific information for athletes—be they Division I, II, or III athletes; athletes in interscholastic programs, athletes in intramural programs; or athletes who just go to the gym a few days a week. For any type of athlete, advice on ways to enhance performance in the athletic arena and in the classroom is given. Student athletes should not have to choose between success in one area and success in another. *Peak performance* is a term used regularly in athletic competition, and often our students do not realize that strategies used for best athletic performance can also be used for best *academic* achievement, and vice versa. Doyle and Zakrajsek apply the science of learning to both areas.

In chapters 2, 3, and 4, special attention is given to helping students understand how changes in their sleep (and nap) habits, the incorporation of exercise into their daily routines, and the use of all of the senses during studying can enhance learning potential, make learning easier, and increase memory. Benefits also include increased patience and self-control. Professors, advisers, and athletic coaches can promote the principles and concepts in this book with their students. In this new edition, Doyle and Zakrajsek have added critical thinking and discussion questions at the end of each chapter. These are invaluable for stimulating self-reflection and thoughtful deliberation as students seek ways to implement the advice and have it become part of their daily habits and routine.

Chapters 5, "Patterns in Learning," and chapter 6, "Memory," are particularity valuable to help students learn how to make sense of new and difficult information. Doyle and Zakrajsek provide insightful and powerful strategies to help students overcome those obstacles to learning and comprehending complex material. Elaboration techniques are explained and methods for becoming self-regulated learners are provided. Best of all, the strategies and techniques are described in useful, practical, and concrete terms so students can start using them right away. At the same time, Doyle and Zakrajsek point out the importance of having a growth mindset toward their learning (chapter 7). In chapter 8, "Paying Attention," Doyle and Zakrajsek continue to foster the notion of students helping themselves by cultivating an attitude of self-reliance and responsibility for their own learning. Learning how to improve attention to detail will empower students' abilities to stay engaged with the learning process, make connections between prior knowledge and new knowledge, and stay positive.

Doyle and Zakrajsek send a powerful message to readers by spelling out information in a logical and compelling manner. They give readers a solid foundation for becoming lifelong learners in a way that is harmonious with the scientific learning. They do not promise a magical transformation with ease, but they do give readers ways to transform their learning capacity by using research-based strategies so that the time and effort spent is worthwhile and rewarding. As Doyle and Zakrajsek point out in the introduction and in the conclusion, "learning is an active process and learning takes work. . . . The one who does the work, does the learning" (p. 16, this volume). Hence, the methods and activities in this book are perfect for students to use when learning so that their time and efforts are maximized.

Kathleen F. Gabriel
Associate Professor
School of Education
California State University, Chico

ACKNOWLEDGMENTS

I want to thank my amazing wife Professor Julie Doyle for the countless hours of discussion we have had about undergraduates and how they learn and what they need to be successful. I want to thank my two brilliant children, Professor Jessica Mekkes and Brendan Doyle, PhD, for sharing their ideas with me about learning and teaching over the past several years. I also want to thank the hundreds of cognitive and neuroscientists for the research they have done, which allows authors like Todd and me to be able to write a book that has the power to really change the way students learn. I want to thank Michael Graham Richard for allowing us to use his work on mindset, which enriched that chapter greatly. I want to thank Gary Bennett for allowing us to use his work on concentration and attention in athletic performance. Finally, I want to thank Alexandra Hartnett and John von Knorring at Stylus Publishing for all their help in bringing this second edition to life.

Terry Doyle

I give credit for almost everything I write to my wife, Debra; my children, Emma, MaryHelen, and Kathryn; and my grandsons, Matthew and Preston. They have listened to endless stories, shared their learning experiences, and been the inspiration for everything important I know about how people learn. Sincere thanks go out to my colleague and good friend, Kathleen Gabriel, for both writing the foreword for this book and engaging me in so many conversations about how best to help students to learn. John von Knorring continues to be a friend and support so much of my professional life. I am indebted to John and Alexandra Hartnett for making this project what it is, as it lies in your hands. Terry and I put much work into the manuscript, but the final product was made so much better by John, Alexandra, and many people at Stylus Publishing. Finally, I thank my students for their eagerness to learn, my colleagues for their willingness to share insights about effective teaching, and university administrators in my life for providing me a safe place to play. The final acknowledgment goes out to you for expanding your mind and working at being even better educated. Learning is a wicked challenge at times, but necessary if we are going to find our way.

Todd Zakrajsek

INTRODUCTION

With so much talk about students who struggle in their classes and how to improve learning in college and university classes, we tend to forget that learning in everyday life is often effortless. Learning isn't confined to the textbooks you read, the lectures you hear, or the class notes you struggle to memorize. You learn all the time without even thinking about it and frequently without even trying. You take short-cuts while walking across campus and learn faster ways to get to certain buildings, you watch movies and learn how police catch serial killers, and you play sports or games and quickly learn who is the best player on the opposing team. At times like these, learning is not something you have to struggle with or spend a lot of time lamenting the diffi-culty of the work. You likely find it fun to learn, and this type of learn-ing happens without even thinking about it. There are other times when learning is difficult and takes a great deal of effort—sometimes in the "real world" and often in your academic studies. You may find it challenging to learn when to apply a new math equation, figure out what your boss really wants in a weekly report, decide which database will work best for a new project at work, or break down complicated plays in a new team sport. It is difficult, but critical, to figure out what makes learning easy some of the time and very difficult at other times. You don't need help learning how to learn when the learning is easy. That you can do on your own. This book is designed to help you learn more about how to learn when the learning is difficult. Notice we said "help you." Nothing can make difficult learning easy, but there are research-based strategies to make it a lot easier. That is what this book is designed to do.

Several thousand years ago, the primary obligation of the human brain was to figure out how to do the things essential to all animals: find food (including differentiating between nutritious and poisonous food), not get eaten by a predator (including finding a safe place to sleep), and reproduce to keep the species alive (typically accomplished by finding a mate). Now, in addition to those basic human functions, our brains are inundated with a multitude of things that need to be learned. Unfortunately, the evolution of the biological structures of the brain does not allow for change as rapid as the pace at which our society is currently changing. Just imagine how much more complicated human life has become in the last 100 years, or just 4 generations. The life you live is massively different in terms of human information processing than the life lived by your great-grandparents when they were your age. College alone is a challenge that many of our great-grandparents never faced. The challenge is that although our world is very different, the brains we were born with are not really any different from those of our great-grandparents. Although our brains have not changed significantly in the past several hundred years, our understanding of how our brains work is light-years ahead of where we were just a few years ago. This new information helps to make sense of the dizzying amount of information we face every day.

New insights into how the human brain learns make it clear that many of the learning practices faculty used in the past, and students continue to use, are highly inefficient, ineffective, or just plain wrong. Worse yet, individuals who get bad grades on tests, or fail to understand a reading, repeat the same bad behaviors they engaged in the first place. Better learning often does not require more effort or more time, but rather effectively aligning how the brain naturally learns with the demands of the college classroom. This book succinctly outlines several easily adapted changes that will significantly enhance your college experience by helping you to learn how to *learn in harmony with your brain*.

Why is it particularly important to learn how to learn as effectively and efficiently as possible? The onslaught of new information, innovation, and challenges facing our world is not going to diminish. College students today face a new world order where global competition for jobs is the norm rather than the exception. India and China have twice as many honor students as the United States has people (Herbold, 2008). These honor students will be seeking the same professional positions that you are seeking. A 2016 study by the Georgetown University Center for Education and the Workplace revealed that those with a bachelor's degree or higher have significantly better employment prospects (and are more likely to get better jobs—those that pay more than $53,000 per year for full-time employment and come with benefits) than those with only a high school diploma or less. Since 2010, 11.6 million new jobs have been created and 99% of those jobs have gone to individuals with some college- or university-level education (Carnevale, Jayasundera, & Gulish, 2016). In addition to being educated to get these jobs, there is no doubt you will need to update your skills and knowledge on a continual basis to keep these jobs. As a result, as a student in college right now you must expect to become a lifelong learner to remain employed. It is essential that you become a highly efficient and effective learner who retains learned knowledge and skills for a lifetime, not just for a test, if you are to compete effectively on the world stage.

This brief book, based on current research about how the human brain learns, will help you to change the ways in which you prepare to learn, make your learning easier and more effective, and improve recall of newly learned material when you need it at a later time. Think about all of the time you are now spending learning new things for your classes. It is ironic that in higher education most individuals spend most of their time learning and very little to no time learning how to learn better. Taking the time to read and reflect on the material in this book will be one of the best decisions you have ever made as a learner. At this point you might be thinking, "There must be a million books out there about how to study and be successful in college." There are many books to teach better study habits and skills, but this is not a book designed to teach you specific study skills, learning strategies, or how to improve your attitude toward learning. This book explains the research about *how* the human brain learns in a way that is easy to understand and act on. This book gives you a foundation on which you can build study skills as needed, but with a much better understanding as to why and how those skills can be best implemented.

As just one example, did you know that neuroscientists have shown that understanding of new material and subsequent recall of that material is enhanced if you don't "stack" your classes so that one occurs right after another? Taking classes back-to-back might help you avoid early courses, reduce your time on campus, or give you one or two days off a week. The problem is that back-to-back classes makes learning much more difficult. Research clearly shows that the human brain needs downtime between different learning experiences in order to process and begin to make new memories of the newly experienced material. The brain needs to work to learn new things, and we need to give it time to undertake the necessary processing. Neuroscientist Lila Davachi of New York University (Tambini, Ketz, & Davachi, 2010) said that "students would be better off taking a coffee break where they just chat with friends for an hour following a college class—it would actually be better for their learning." Strategic downtime to avoid overloading the brain processing a lot of new unrelated material, when not overdone, is an effective part of the learning process.

The authors of this book have a singular goal for anyone reading: to better understand *how you can learn how to learn in harmony with your brain!* It is not difficult to make the changes suggested in this book. But it is critical. Becoming a skilled and efficient learner will be one of the most important determinants of what you can and will achieve in your lifetime. Our purpose in writing this book is to help you reach your full potential by providing you a simple way to understand the learning process.

A Special Note to the Reader

We have purposefully written each chapter of this book as a standalone introduction to a specific aspect of the human brain. As a result, some information is repeated in multiple chapters because it relates to the topic in that chapter or an activity under discussion. For example, making new memories is affected by sleep (chapter 2), exercise (chapter 3), attention (chapter 8), and practice and elaboration (chapter 6). We believe the repetition will serve to reinforce important information about learning and that you will find it helpful to consider the information in multiple ways.

Critical Thinking and Discussion Questions

1. Briefly describe one thing you have learned in the past week that was easy and one thing you learned in the past week that was difficult. How did these two things differ from one another? Why was one easy and the other difficult? Don't simply say, "Because I liked one more than the other." Think about why one was easier than the other.

2. What is one strategy that you have used regularly that you feel helps you to learn? Ask three different people to describe one strategy that each uses. How are your strategies similar to and different from their strategies? For those strategies that are different, why might their strategies work or not work for you?

3. Read one published article that addresses the concept of how people learn. Note whether this is a research article or a popular press article and why that might be important. Identify one strategy or concept from the article that you can implement into your own learning. After trying this strategy a few times explain whether, or to what extent, this strategy or concept facilitates your learning.

References

Carnevale, A. P., Jayasundera, T., & Gulish, A. (2016). *America's divided recovery: College haves and have-nots.* Washington DC: Georgetown University Center for Education and the Workforce. Retrieved from https://cew-7632.kxcdn.com/wp-content/uploads/Americas-Divided-Recovery-web.pdf

Herbold, R. (2008, December). Does the U.S. realize it's in competition? *Think*. Retrieved from http://www.case.edu/magazine/springsummer 2010/competition.htm

Tambini, A., Ketz, N., & Davachi, L. (2010). Enhanced brain correlations during rest are related to memory for recent experiences. *Neuron, 65*(2), 280–290.

1

A NEW LOOK AT LEARNING

We are all constantly learning, from the day we are born until the day we die. We learn how to tie our shoes, the best route to the mall, which friends can be trusted with a secret, how to find the area of a circle, and which teachers will accept late papers in class. We learn which TV programs we like, how to write a strong introductory paragraph, what makes our friends angry, when a faculty member is likely to give a pop quiz, and who has the best burgers. When we're awake it is rare not to be learning. Given the wide variety of learning everyone does, it is surprising that schools do not regularly teach individuals how to learn. Even faculty members who have spent their entire lives in the educational system and obtain a PhD rarely consult the vast literature on how people learn or have taken "how to learn" classes. If you are in college, or in high school and heading off to college in the future, you certainly are good at learning, but knowing the research behind which strategies, and under which circumstances, bring about the most learning is something that can benefit anyone. That is the primary purpose of this book. This is the second edition of *The New Science of Learning: How to Learn in Harmony With Your Brain*. In the first edition of this book we demonstrated it was possible to write an easy-to-read, research-based book on this topic. The book we wrote was possible because 20 years ago scientists began to develop highly effective tools that allow us today to get a much better understanding of how the most complicated system ever known—the human brain—operates. A lot has changed in just the past 5 years. Although much of the foundational information remains the same as when we wrote the first edition, advanced technology has allowed scientists to see even more of the brain and how it functions, resulting in a better understanding of what it all means. Of course, there are still many areas yet to be discovered and neuroscience is still far from providing a complete understanding of how the brain works. However, nearly a decade ago, at a 2010 meeting of neuroscience experts Dr. James Bibb of the University of Texas Southwestern Medical Center said, "We have accumulated enough knowledge about the mechanisms and molecular underpinnings of cognition at the synaptic and circuit levels to say something about which processes contribute" (Bibb, 2010). Bibb expanded on his statement in a 2010 article in the *Journal of Neuroscience*, in which he and his coauthors indicated that there is finally enough understanding about how learning happens to suggest that the process is wholly different from what most students imagine (Bibb, Mayford, Tsien, & Alberini, 2010). Research continues to emerge that places us on the front edge of being able to even better facilitate learning abilities. In this second edition of the book, we will share the newest findings in cognitive neuroscience to help you to **learn in harmony with your brain.**

A New Definition of *Learning*

What does it mean to say you have learned something?

Neuroscientist researchers have shown that when you learn something new, there is a physical change in your brain. You have approximately 86 billion neurons in your brain (Randerson, 2012), and each neuron can form up to 10,000 connections with other neurons, meaning we have somewhere around 40 quadrillion (40,000,000,000,000,000) total connections in our brains (Ratey, 2001). Our brains are adapting all the time, with unused connections fading away and new connections and networks being formed when new information is learned. When frequently activated and practiced, these new networks have the potential to form long-term memories. In fact, every time you use or practice newly learned information or skills the connections between the brain cells get stronger and your ability to recall the information also becomes easier and faster. Establishing new connections is like blazing a trail through a thick forest, which is a great deal of work. But every time that trail is used it becomes more established and easier and faster to follow. At the level of neurons, this process of establishing and then maintaining the trail is called "long-term potentiation" (Ratey, 2001, p. 191). As a result of long-term potentiation, something that was at one time new to you and took much effort becomes routine and very easy. Your multiplication tables or the lines from a poem that were once a challenge become more routine and take less and less cognitive effort. Long-term potentiation is a neurological description of how habits and long-term memories are formed. Knowledge and skills practiced enough become a more permanent part of your memory and will be easily available to you when you need them, even if you don't need them for weeks, months, or perhaps even years later.

The important message for all learners is that new learning requires a considerable amount of practice and effort to make meaningful connections to other information and to become a more permanent part of memory. Learning can be hard work, and you should expect to find yourself tired at the end of the day when learning a lot of new material. Although there are some shortcuts and methods to make learning more efficient, never underestimate the energy consumed by your brain when you learn. As challenging and exhausting as it may be to learn when you really enjoy the material, you know it is even more difficult to learn when you either don't want to learn or are disengaged from the material. Neuroscience researchers have made it clear that learning is an active process and learning takes work. The more work you do with something that you are learning, and the more ways you engage with it—such as listening, talking, reading, writing, reviewing, or thinking about it—the stronger the connections in your brain become and the more likely the new learning will become a more permanent memory. An additional finding from neuroscience research is that to form lasting memories, practice typically needs to happen over extended periods of time. Psychologists have studied this phenomenon, called the *distributed practice effect*, for more than 100 years (Aaron & Tullis, 2010; Ebbinghaus, 1913). This building and strengthening can take many forms, but the process is similar in that distributed practice is crucial to learning. If you want to build strong muscles for a football game think how ridiculous it would be to do weight-training cramming sessions. Imagine once a week you did a 5- to 7-hour lifting session the night before the game. Or if you had a race to run and you crammed all your running practices into the day before the race, expecting to then do well in the race. If you really want to be stronger or faster, you practice a bit every day across time. You would also expect to be tired after each practice session. The same is true for your brain. To build strong areas of knowledge, distributed practice is important. Then you need to keep what you have gained. If you get into shape and then stop exercising, muscle strength and lung capacity fade. Learning that is not periodically used faces the same outcome. When you have learned something new, if you don't practice what you have learned, the information will likely fade. Learning, like exercise, is very much a use-it-or-lose-it proposition.

All this new research in neuroscience has led to a completely new way of thinking about the teaching and learning process in school. It is called learning-centered teaching (LCT). Not all teachers are using LCT, but every year more do, and every indication suggests that is certainly the direction in which higher education will continue to go. In the LCT model, your teacher's goal is to get you to do as much of the work in the learning process as possible, because the more work your brain does, the more connections will be established, which increases the likelihood for more permanent memories to be formed. This new LCT approach is often uncomfortable for students who are used to having the teacher tell them what to learn and then memorizing it a day or two before the test. The discomfort usually comes in the form of being asked to do more work and to take a more active role in the classroom, rather than just listening to a lecture. LCT does not do away with lecture, but rather pairs lectures with teaching and learning strategies that help students to do some of the work of learning (Harrington & Zakrajsek, 2017; Major, Harris, & Zakrajsek, 2015). As you do more of the work of learning and engage in more regular practice of what you have been asked to learn, long-term potentiation will kick in, and like a learning trail that you have already blazed, you will start remembering the new learning more easily and for a much longer period. As with following a blazed trail, learning will also become easier and require less and less energy. This will allow you to think about and learn even more complex material.

Preparing to Learn—Nutrition, Hydration, Sleep, and Exercise

One of the most important new insights into how the human brain learns is that it needs to be ready and able to learn if it is to work at its best. Showing up to class without proper sleep, without regular exercise, and without eating or hydrating will cause your brain to operate inefficiently, making learning even more difficult.

Nutrition

The human brain uses 25% to 30% of the body's energy—in the form of glucose—every day (Armstrong, 2017). This means if you do not have a healthy diet and eat regular balanced meals, you are starving your brain of the energy it needs to function properly, causing your brain to work much less efficiently. A brain starved for glucose is a brain not ready to learn, meaning more effort with less result. The brain does much better if the blood glucose level can be held relatively stable. To do this, avoid simple carbohydrates containing sugar and white flour (e.g., pastries, white bread, and pasta). Rely on the complex carbohydrates found in fruits, whole grains, and vegetables. Protein is also important; instead of starting your day with coffee and a donut, try tea and an egg on wheat toast, and take a multivitamin every day (Hallowell, 2005). It is valuable to constantly experiment with food choices while you learn and find what works best for you. Most individuals notice it is easier to learn new information when maintaining a balanced diet. As with your car, your brain needs fuel to run, and the better the fuel the more efficiently it runs. Most individuals simply never think about how food relates to learning, but research shows us it is crucial that you eat properly before you try to learn.

Hydration

In addition to needing food, your brain also needs to stay hydrated. Neurons (brain cells) store water in tiny balloon-like structures called vacuoles. Water is essential for optimal brain health and function. Water is necessary for the brain's cognitive processes to work at their most efficient and effective levels (Masento, Golightly, Field, Butler, & van Reekum, 2014). Dehydration often leads to fatigue, dizziness, poor concentration, and reduced cognitive abilities. Even mild levels of dehydration have been shown to negatively impact school performance (Norman, 2012). When you wake up each morning you may not be aware that you are very likely dehydrated. Think about it; you have not had any liquid intake for 6 to 10 hours and the body loses a significant amount of water (as much as two pounds of water) while sleeping (Krulwich, 2013). It is simply not enough to wake up, grab your clothes, and head to class. You need to prepare your brain to learn by feeding and hydrating it; otherwise, you are making learning much more difficult for yourself.

Staying properly hydrated throughout the day is a bit of a balancing act. Although too little water can make thinking and learning difficult, too much water can be harmful (Kim, 2012). The best advice is to drink when thirsty and to drink water whenever possible. Also, eat foods that are high in water composition (e.g., watermelon, grapes, and raw fruits). Be cautious about drinking too many caffeinated beverages as these can interfere with your sleep, especially if you consume them after 6:00 p.m. Research shows that caffeinated beverages actually do not dehydrate you, as is commonly believed, but they can interfere with getting a good night's sleep (Armstrong et al., 2005).

Sleep and Exercise

Brain research has produced overwhelming evidence of the importance exercise and sleep play in the brain's ability to learn and remember. We see these two areas as so important that we have devoted chapters to each of them. Chapter 2, "Sleep, Naps, and Breaks," covers a wide range of vital information about the relationship between a good night's rest and effective learning and the making of long-term memories, which are the key to college success. Chapter 3, "Exercise and Learning," discusses the profound effect exercise has on improving learning and memory. Exercise and sleep are often overlooked for their impact on learning, and yet they likely contribute more than anything else to your ability to learn.

Preparing the brain to learn is a new idea for most students, but it is crucial to your ability to learn. A tired, hungry, and thirsty brain deprived of the vital benefits of exercise is a brain not ready to learn.

Cramming Is a Learning Trap

We refer to cramming as a learning trap because the practice of cramming can result in doing well on an individual test or quiz, but it has terrible outcomes for long-term retention of the material learned (Ellis, 2015). Because cramming can result in short-term gains on unit quizzes and exams, it makes cramming look effective, yet it is not. It is highly likely you have crammed for an exam at some point, and you already know how quickly the information is forgotten. What is not often considered is that later in the semester, say before the final exam, when the information is needed, you have to start the learning process all over again. The same is true when you need the information months, or even years, later at work. This is why people will often talk about what they learned in college, and yet find it hard to apply much of that information to their job. Another drawback to cramming is that sometimes you get confused by all the last-minute information. Finally, cramming typically leads to a lack of sleep, which then leads to simple mistakes that you would not make if you were better rested. Being fatigued makes trying to recall information that is not well established much more difficult and increases the chance of confusion between all the facts just learned.

The fact is that the practice of cramming does not meet the neuroscience definition of *learning*. The definition of *learning* requires that information be available for use at a later time. Forming permanent memories comes from distributed practice over time; cramming typically does not allow the brain to do the work it needs to do to establish more permanent memories by building a strong connection to the new material. So, technically, cramming does not typically result in real learning. You can cram the night before the exam and then relearn the material later when it is needed for the final, in another course, or on the job, but that involves a lot of extra time and effort. A more effective approach is to learn it correctly the first time and then later have the material available to you (perhaps at your new job) with a very quick review. Again, this is why cramming is an academic trap; you might reinforce this behavior by doing well on a unit exam the next day, but then all that work is lost when you can't mentally access the information at a later time.

Transference of Learning

You can demonstrate learning when you use existing information to help you learn similar new information; that is, when you apply the new information to problems beyond those you have been doing in class. Psychologists call this learning transference (Barnett & Ceci, 2002). Transference is the principle at work when the questions on your math test are different from the questions you did in class or were given as homework. The closer the transfer distance, the less you need to really understand what you are doing. It is relatively easy to memorize and then "transfer" the information to something almost identical. Real learning happens when you start to increase the distance of the transfer. As problems to be solved become increasingly different from what you learned in class, your instructor is trying to help you to really understand the math by seeing if you can employ your understanding to solve new problems using the knowledge you developed on the problems you have been solving.

Life won't give you the exact same problems all the time, and knowing how to apply information to solve new problems is the foundation of being educated. Memorized information might help on a low-level test, but it won't help much in life unless you get on

Jeopardy! Look for connections between learned material and new material, and celebrate any time you see you have transferred information, particularly when there is a fairly big difference. Transference of knowledge and skills will both help you ace the final and do well at your future job. That said, learning to transfer new learning is not easy, despite its importance. It also typically requires a bit of extra practice. Long-term potentiation really helps facilitate transfer. (By the way, if you understand that last sentence you have already learned a lot and currently know more than most about learning in harmony with your brain.)

The Brain Looks to Connect to What Has Already Been Learned

The human brain is constantly looking for connections. Connections help you use prior knowledge to build bridges to the new material, creating a more meaningful understanding of the new material. Have you ever noticed how easy it is to remember someone's name after meeting for the first time if that person looks a bit like someone you know with the same name? If you have played music for a long time, you have also seen this in action. You likely find it much easier to learn new music when you recognize many of the patterns and can connect them to music you already know. Yes, that is also why you had to spend all that time at the beginning learning musical scales. What is great about how the brain works when learning new material is that the more you learn, the easier it is to learn.

Some subjects are more difficult for you to learn because you lack prior knowledge, not because you lack intelligence. Lack of knowledge makes it difficult for your brain to figure out how to make connections with information already known. Everyone accepted into college has the intellectual capabilities necessary to graduate if they are willing to put in the time and effort. The key to successfully dealing with difficult new material is a willingness to get help filling in the missing prior knowledge when you need it and then practicing the new learning enough to make more permanent memories of it. Unfortunately, many students think they are not smart enough to learn the difficult material, which is a complete misunderstanding of how the human brain works. We all get smarter every day by adding to our knowledge and skill base. From there we make new connections that allow us to learn even more. The more you learn about something, the easier it is to learn about that thing.

The key to handling difficult subjects is to fill in the background information that you may not have learned in your earlier schooling so that your brain can have something to connect the new knowledge to. If you fill in these knowledge gaps, then your success will depend entirely on the amount of practice you are willing to put in to master a subject. It is true that some people have greater abilities in certain areas, but if you have been accepted into college, you have already demonstrated the abilities necessary to handle the subjects you will be asked to learn. College success does not depend on being smart; it is about learning how to be an effective learner. While learning something difficult, resist telling yourself that "you can't do it"; instead, tell yourself that "you can't do it yet."

Athletes and Learning

As the authors of this book, we're conscious of the applicability of the ideas in this book to learning outside the classroom to the extent that we have included a section in each chapter on the application of the chapter's message to athletic performance. By athletes we mean anyone who engages in regular physical activity—whether you just work out at the gym three days a week, play intramurals, dance, swim, jog, or play a college sport. If you're engaging in athletic performance and want to learn how to become more skilled, efficient, or strategic, applying what you learn in the following chapters can help.

The Key Message

The primary message from neuroscience researchers is relatively simple: "It is the one who does the work does the learning" (Doyle, 2008, p. 63). Only when you do the practicing, reading, writing, thinking, talking, collaborating, and reflecting does your brain make more permanent connections. Your teachers cannot do this for you, and, at times, this work will make you tired. When that happens, rest a bit and reflect on the fact that you are changing the neurochemistry in your brain. That is pretty amazing.

Chapter Summary

There is new understanding about how learning happens, and this new understanding contradicts what most students think happens when they learn. You need to know the findings in order to maximize your learning abilities. Following are the key ideas from this chapter:

1. Neuroscience research shows that when you learn something new, there is a physical change in your brain. You have approximately 86 billion brain cells, and when you learn something new some of your brain cells establish connections with other brain cells to form new networks of cells, which actually represent the new learning that has taken place.
2. Every time you use or practice newly learned information or skills the connections among the brain cells get stronger and your ability to recall the information also becomes faster. This is called long-term potentiation.
3. The important message for all learners is that new learning requires a considerable amount of practice and a meaningful connection to other information in order to become a permanent part of memory.
4. Neuroscience research has also found that to form lasting memories, practice needs to happen over extended periods. Psychologists call this the distributed practice effect.
5. Cramming is not learning. The definition of *learning* requires information to be "relatively permanent" and for the brain to form more permanent memories. A day or two of cramming is not nearly enough.

6. Learning requires that you are able to use newly acquired information in new ways, a process psychologists call transference.

7. The human brain is constantly looking for connections to prior knowledge. These connections link previously learned material to new material, creating a more meaningful understanding of the new material.

8. The message from neuroscience researchers is a simple one, as noted previously: The one who does the work does the learning (Doyle, 2008). Only when you do the practicing, reading, writing, thinking, talking, collaborating, and reflecting does your brain make more permanent connections. Your teachers cannot do this for you.

Critical Thinking and Discussion Questions

1. Define *long-term potentiation* in your own words and give three examples based on your own learning. How does long-term potentiation relate to learning foundational material in any course?

2. Think of something that you do extremely well right now. How did you get so good or knowledgeable at what you have listed? Have you found that as you learn more learning becomes easier and perhaps even more enjoyable? How similar is that learning process to what you do when learning new information in your classes?

3. The authors call cramming a "learning trap." Explain how this trap might work in a class you are taking this semester. Find two different friends who regularly cram for exams. Ask them if they think the material stays with them and what impact this way of studying has on their final exams. What can you do to stay out of this trap?

4. Why do the authors keep talking about how much work it is to learn? Is all learning difficult? If not, what makes some learning more effortful than other learning?

5. What do you find to be most difficult about learning? Based on this chapter, what might you try to make it just a little bit easier or less painful?

References

Aaron, S., & Tullis, J. (2010, November). What makes distributed practice effective? *Cognitive Psychology, 61*(3), 228–247.

Armstrong, L. (2017, August 14). The roles of glucose in the brain [Web log post]. Retrieved from https://www.livestrong.com/article/358622-the-roles-of-glucose-in-the-brain/

Armstrong, L. E., Pumerantz, A. C., Roti, M. W., Judelson, D. A., Watson, G., Dias, J. C., . . . Kellogg, M. (2005, June). Fluid, electrolyte, and renal indices of hydration during 11 days of controlled caffeine consumption. *International Journal of Sport Nutrition and Exercise Metabolism, 15*(3), 252–265.

Barnett, S. M., & Ceci, S. J. (2002). When and where do we apply what we learn? A taxonomy for far transfer. *Psychological Bulletin, 128*, 612–637.

Bibb, J. (2010). *Cognitive enhancement strategies.* Presentation given at the 2010 meeting of the Society of Neuroscience, San Diego, CA.

Bibb, J., Mayford, A., Tsien, J., & Alberini, C. (2010, November 10). Cognition enhancement strategies. *The Journal of Neuroscience, 30*(45), 14987–14992.

Doyle, T. (2008). *Helping students learn in a learner-centered environment.* Sterling, VA: Stylus.

Ebbinghaus, H. (1913). *A contribution to experimental psychology.* New York, NY: Teachers College, Columbia University.

Ellis, D. (2015). *Becoming a master student.* Stamford, CT: Cengage Learning.

Hallowell, E. (2005, January). Overloaded circuits: Why smart people underperform. *Harvard Business Review.* Retrieved from https://hbr.org/2005/01/overloaded-circuits-why-smart-people-underperform

Harrington, C., & Zakrajsek, T. (2017). *Dynamic lecturing: Research-based strategies to enhance lecture effectiveness.* Sterling, VA: Stylus.

Kim, B. (2012, June 11). Why drinking too much water can be harmful to your health [Web log post]. Retrieved from http://drbenkim.com/drink-too-much-water-dangerous.html

Krulwich, R. (2013, June 21). Every night you lose more than a pound while you're asleep (for the oddest reason) [Web log post]. Retrieved from https://www.npr.org/sections/krulwich/2013/06/19/193556929/every-night-you-lose-more-than-a-pound-while-youre-asleep-for-the-oddest-reason

Major, C., Harris, M., & Zakrajsek, T. (2015). *Teaching for learning: 101: Intentionally designed teaching activities to put students on the path to success.* Sterling, VA: Stylus.

Masento, N. A., Golightly, M., Field, D. T., Butler, L. T., & van Reekum, C. M. (2014). Effects of hydration status on cognitive performance and mood. *British Journal of Nutrition, 111*(10), 1841–1852.

Norman, P. (2012, July 23). Dehydration: Its impact on learning. *Ashburn Patch.* Retrieved from https://patch.com/virginia/ashburn/bp--dehydration-its-impact-on-learning

Randerson, J. (2012, February 28). How many neurons make a human brain? Billions fewer than we thought [Web log post]. *The Guardian.* Retrieved from https://www.theguardian.com/science/blog/2012/feb/28/how-many-neurons-human-brain

Ratey, J. (2001). *A user's guide to the brain.* New York, NY: Pantheon.

2

SLEEP, NAPS, AND BREAKS

Would you be interested in a proven, extensively researched, and amazing treatment that makes you live longer; enhances your memory; makes you more attractive; helps you to lose weight (or stay slim); reduces your chances of getting diabetes; decreases the chance of cancer and dementia; lowers your risk of getting sick; and also makes you feel better, happier, and less anxious? How about if this treatment was also painless and free from cost? It does exist! It is sleep! There are thousands of studies that support every claim made in this opening paragraph (Walker, 2017).

In a 2017 *New York Times* article "Sleep Is the New Status Symbol," internationally recognized sleep scientist Matthew Walker said, according to the World Health Organization and the National Sleep Foundation, sleep is the single most effective thing we can do to reset our brain and body health each day (Walker, 2017, April 8). So how many hours of sleep did you get last night? The night before that? When college students are asked about sleep, most report not getting enough. What has your life looked like over the past week? Right now, as you read this book, do you feel tired or rested? We all know that it is more difficult to learn something new when tired, but the role of sleep and fatigue involves more than having difficulty focusing or staying awake when studying.

Sleep affects every aspect of your being. Sleep enhances your ability to learn, memorize, and make logical decisions and choices about your learning. Sleep improves your psychological health and the recalibration of your emotional brain circuits that enable you to navigate the challenges you face each day with unruffled composure. Sleep restocks your immune system, allowing it to fight off sickness; regulates your appetite; maintains the microbiome in your gut where nutrition health begins; and aids in maintaining the health of your cardiovascular system (Walker, 2017).

Research on sleep has made it clear that the time, money, and effort you put into learning the content and skills in your courses is significantly compromised by lack of sleep. Adults typically need 7.5 to 9 hours of sleep each night to feel fully rested and function at their best. Those still in their teen years need 9 to 10 hours per night.

According to a 2016 report from the U.S. Centers for Disease Control and Prevention (CDC), one of every three Americans doesn't get enough sleep on a regular basis. About 35% of U.S. adults are sleeping less than 7 hours a night, increasing their risk of a wide variety of health problems. Getting less than 7 hours of sleep a night is associated with increased risk of obesity, type-2 diabetes, high blood pressure, heart disease, stroke, mental distress, and death (CDC, 2016). Research from Hershner and Chevin (2014) found 50% of college students report daytime sleepiness and 70% obtain insufficient sleep. Furthermore, 18% of college men and 30% of college women report having suffered from insomnia in the past 3 months. Sleep deprivation in students has also been linked to lower grade point averages (GPAs), as sleep affects concentration, memory, and the ability to learn (Campus Mind Works, 2016).

Despite greater awareness of the importance of sleep, Americans are getting less sleep than they did in the past. A 2015 National Sleep Foundation (NSF) poll found that about two-thirds (63%) of Americans say their sleep needs are not being met during the week. Most of the individuals responding to the poll indicated needing about 7.5 hours of sleep to feel their best, but they report getting an average of 6 hours and 55 minutes of sleep on weeknights. The situation with the lack of sleep is so bad that in 2014 the CDC declared sleep deprivation a public health epidemic.

What Researchers Say About Sleep

Sleep is an important part of your daily routine—you spend about one-third of your time doing it. Quality sleep, and getting enough of it at the right times, is as essential to survival as food and water. Without sleep, you can't form or maintain the pathways in your brain that let you learn and create new memories, and it's harder to concentrate and respond quickly (National Institute of Neurological Disorders and Stroke, 2017). Neuroscientist Matthew Walker, former director of the Beth Israel Deaconess Medical Center's Sleep and Neuroimaging Laboratory, said, "You can't short-change your brain of sleep and still learn effectively" (cited in Beth Israel Deaconess Medical Center, 2005, para. 16). So, if you are not getting 7.5 to 9 hours of sleep each night, you are likely sabotaging your own learning.

Sleep and Memory

György Buzsáki, professor at the Center for Molecular and Behavioral Neuroscience at Rutgers University, and his co-researchers have determined that short transient brain events, called sharp wave ripples, are responsible for consolidating memories and transferring new information from the hippocampus, which is a fast-learning but low-capacity short-term memory store, to the neocortex, which is a slower learning but higher capacity long-term memory store (Buzsáki, Girardeau, Benchenane, Wiener, & Zugaro, 2009). Information stored in the neocortex and regularly used or retrieved becomes more stable and has a greater likelihood of becoming a long-term memory (see Figure 2.1). Buzsáki and his colleagues also found that this transference of information happens primarily when we are asleep (Rutgers University, 2009).

Sleep Patterns

There are three distinct sleep patterns: REM (rapid eye movement) sleep, light NREM (non-REM), and deep NREM. Deep NREM is also called slow-wave sleep. If your alarm (or a person) wakes you up and you are very groggy and confused, it is likely that you were in an

Figure 2.1. Sleep helps memory traces to move from the hippocampus to the neocortex, where they are more stable.

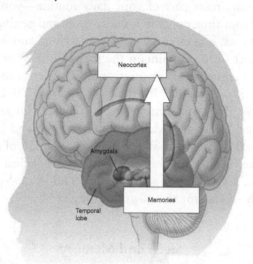

Source: From www.positscience.com. ©1999 by Scientific Learning Corporation. Reprinted with permission.

NREM deep state of sleep. This slower and deeper level of sleep typically takes place primarily earlier in the night. REM sleep occurs more frequently later in the night. Current research shows that during slow-wave sleep your brain works on making memories for motor skills and for declarative types of information, such as facts or new vocabulary words (Walker, 2017). During REM sleep the brain makes procedural memories or memories of skills like how to write a research paper, dissect a frog, or dribble a basketball. In addition, during slow-wave sleep the body repairs cells, tissues, and muscles, and heals any wounds, injuries, or illnesses (Walker, 2017). While in REM sleep the brain takes newly learned information and searches every corner of your memory to find connections to your prior knowledge. Sometimes the brain makes connections to things you never thought of while awake. This is why sleep can produce new insights and creative solutions to problems you had not considered, leading to enhanced understanding of newly learned material (Walker, 2017).

Sleep also serves other functions. In addition to providing an opportunity to consolidate memories and heal the body and brain, sleep allows your brain to clear space for new learning to occur the next day. Memory researcher Matthew Walker and his co-researchers have shown that during sleep 12-Hz to 14-Hz bursts of brain waves, called sleep spindles, network between key regions of the brain to clear a path for new learning (Walker & Robertson, 2016). These electrical impulses, which fire at a rate of 15 to 20 per second, help to shift memories from the brain's hippocampus—which, as stated earlier, has limited storage space—to the nearly limitless prefrontal cortex's "hard drive," thus freeing up the hippocampus to take in fresh data (new learning). In a very real sense, while you learn during the day you are sending information directly to your hippocampus, so it needs to be cleared each night for new learning to take place the next day.

Walker says sleep is the key to having a brain that is ready to learn ("Naps Clear the Mind," 2010). Bryce Mander, a postdoctoral fellow in psychology at the University of California, Berkeley, and lead author of a study on sleep spindles, adds, "A lot of that spindle-rich sleep is occurring [during] the second half of the night, so if you sleep 6 hours or less, you are shortchanging yourself and impeding your learning" (American Association for the Advancement of Science, 2011). The study's coauthor Matthew Walker went on to say, "This discovery indicates that we not only need sleep after learning to consolidate what we've learned, but that we also need to be rested before learning, so that we can recharge and soak up new information the next day" (American Association for the Advancement of Science, 2011).

Why Sleep Is Crucial to Learning and Memory

"When you're asleep, your brain shifts memories to more efficient storage regions within the brain. When you awaken, you find memory tasks can be performed both more quickly and accurately and with less stress and anxiety" (Walker & Robertson, 2016). Sleep protects new memories from disruption by the interfering experiences that are inevitable during wakefulness (Payne et al., 2012). An important finding by Wilhelm and his co-researchers is that during sleep memories are consolidated according to their relative importance, based on your expectations (wanting to remember is vital to memory formation) for remembering (Wilhelm et al., 2011). Later in this chapter we will discuss in more detail the importance of wanting to remember.

The three key messages here are, first, new learning is quite fragile and susceptible to change and interference before it is consolidated. REM and slow-wave sleep help to consolidate memories. Second, in research by Payne and colleagues (2012), it was reported that sleeping soon after learning benefits both episodic memory (events) and semantic memory (facts about the world). This means that it would be a good thing to rehearse any information you need to remember immediately before you go to bed. Third, it seems that when you tell the brain what to consolidate it does a better job of keeping these memories (Payne et al., 2012). You facilitate consolidation through the information you pay attention to and what you practice, think about, read, write, and study. The information and skills you use send a message to the brain that these are important and should be kept as memories. Failing to do these kinds of studying activities signals the brain the opposite—that this information is not important and can be done away with. When it comes to the brain and learning, wanting to remember is an important step.

Three Stages of Memory Processing

The three stages of memory processing are encoding, storage, and retrieval. All three are affected in different ways by the amount of sleep you get. It is difficult to encode new learning when you are tired and unable to pay attention to the information. When you are sleep deprived, the longer you are awake, the more difficult it is to learn new information. Similarly, without the proper amount of sleep, storage of new memories is disrupted.

The third stage of memory processing is the retrieval (recall) state. During retrieval, the memory is accessed and re-edited. This is often the most important stage, as learned material is of limited value if it can't be recalled when needed, which of course would also be important during an exam. Maas and Robbins (2011) write that recall is impeded by a lack of sleep. Converging scientific evidence, from the molecular

BOX 2.1
The Stages of Sleep

Non-REM sleep

Stage N1 (transition to sleep)—This stage lasts about 5 minutes. Your eyes move slowly under your eyelids, muscle activity slows down, and you are easily awakened.

Stage N2 (light sleep)—This is the first stage of true sleep, lasting 10 to 25 minutes. Eye movement stops, heart rate slows, and body temperature decreases.

Stage N3 (deep sleep)—You're difficult to awaken, and if you are awakened, you do not adjust immediately and often feel groggy and disoriented for several minutes. In this deepest stage of sleep, your brain waves are extremely slow. Blood flow is directed away from your brain and toward your muscles, restoring physical energy.

REM sleep

REM sleep (dream sleep)—About 70 to 90 minutes after falling asleep, you enter REM sleep, the stage during which dreaming occurs. Your eyes move rapidly, your breathing becomes shallow, and your heart rate and blood pressure increase. Also during this stage, your arm and leg muscles are paralyzed.

Source: Smith, Robinson, & Segal, 2013.

to the phenomenological, leaves little doubt that memory reprocessing "offline" (i.e., during sleep; see Box 2.1), is an important component of how our memories are formed, shaped, and recalled (Stickgold, 2015).

Sleep Patterns—Larks, Night Owls, and the Rest of Us

Humans differ on many dimensions. Sleep is no exception. Individuals vary in the amounts of sleep they need. In the absence of alcohol, drugs, or sleep challenges, the most important measure of the proper amount of sleep is simply how you feel. If you are fatigued, then you need more sleep, even if you regularly sleep 8 hours per night. If you feel rested sleeping 6 hours per night, that is all the sleep you may need, although few people can sleep an average of only 6 hours and feel rested. Individuals also differ on the time of day during which they function at an optimal level. For some, early morning is the best time for serious learning, whereas others learn best late at night. Current research clearly shows people have definite differences in their sleep patterns. According to Matthew Walker (2017), 40% of the adult population is made up of larks (morning people). These people are at their best for learning in the morning to mid-afternoon. They go to bed earlier and get up earlier. Approximately 30% of the adult population are night owls. They are at their best in the afternoon into the late evening. They stay up late and get up late. The rest of the population are in between but have a slight lean toward the owls.

These variations in sleep patterns, or chronotypes, are a result of our genes, and although our sleep patterns can change as our lives and work schedules change, the process is not often easy to deal with ("Genes Linked," 2011). Jim Wilson, author of the University of Edinburgh's Centre for Population Health Sciences study of sleep patterns, found that a tendency to sleep for longer or shorter periods often runs in families, although the amount of sleep people need is also influenced by age, latitude, season, and circadian (24-hour cycle) rhythms ("Genes Linked," 2011).

If you are most alert around noon each day, do your best work in the hours before you eat lunch, and are ready for bed relatively early each night, you are definitively a morning person, or lark. Knowing you are a lark is important information from the standpoint of learning. Larks are much better off taking classes, doing more challenging homework, and studying during the morning or daytime hours and leaving their easier work and socializing until night, when they are likely more tired.

If you are most alert around 6:00 p.m., do your best work late in the evening, and often stay up until 2:00 a.m. or 3:00 a.m., you are a night owl. Night owls who take morning classes tend to have more difficulty staying awake and paying attention simply because their natural rhythms identify the early morning as a time to sleep, not be in class. If you are a night owl, sign up for afternoon classes and plan to do challenging homework and study later in the evening. Being a night owl is a normal part of your brain's makeup. Unfortunately, our society does not recognize this and often sees people who are owls as lazy because they are sleepy in the morning hours when jobs typically begin. Companies would get much better work from their owls if they allowed them to work a schedule fitting their natural sleep cycle.

In a 2008 study involving more than 800 students, Kendry Clay of the University of North Texas found that college students who were night owls had lower GPAs than those who were larks. One reason for this discrepancy was the great likelihood that the night owls were sleep deprived (American Academy of Sleep Medicine, 2008). A 2013 study by Gillen-O'Neel, Fuligni, and Huynh at University of California, Los Angeles (UCLA), involving 535 students found that those who didn't get enough sleep were not only more likely to have problems understanding during class, a result the researchers had expected, but also more likely to do worse on tests, quizzes, and homework, often leading to significantly lower overall GPAs. For suggestions for changing your sleep pattern to get enough sleep, see Box 2.2.

It is also important to note that about 30% of the adult population does not fall into either the lark or night owl category. If you do not tend to get up very early or stay up very late, you simply need to identify your best time of the day for learning.

Most people have not thought carefully about how to structure their day to optimize their learning time according to natural rhythms. One way to do this is to keep a log for one week. Find or make a chart that starts Sunday night at 6:00 p.m. and has blocks for the 24 hours of each day. Each day when you wake up, color in the blocks to show the time you slept the night before. Then, periodically through the day, rate yourself based on how mentally alert you feel. Your self-assigned ratings will vary greatly based on what you are doing, but over time you will likely see patterns. If you read a chapter of a book and feel like you understood it very well, give yourself an A, for "alert," during that

BOX 2.2
Recommendations for Changing Night Owl Sleep Patterns

Researchers have shown time and again that it is possible to adjust your sleep and lead a healthier and more productive life. Following are a few common tips to establish better sleep health:

- Avoid all-nighters and cramming for exams through the night. It is much healthier to complete the most difficult studying in the morning, when your brain is more fresh and alert. Schedule study sessions that include other individuals in the afternoon and early evening when possible.
- Make good food and beverage choices before sleeping. Beer and pizza are both bad for sleep. Alcohol disrupts sleep, and heavy caloric foods just prior to sleeping are both bad for your quality of sleep and will lead to weight gain. Keep in mind that caffeine and alcohol often take 6 hours to be processed and removed from the body. It is helpful to plan carefully to eat and drink appropriately in the hours before sleeping.
- Establish a good sleep cycle. As much as possible, go to bed at the same time every night and try to wake up at the same time each day. That will train your body and result in better sleep.
- Bedtime routines help signal to the brain that it is time to go to sleep. You may be too old for warm milk and a bedtime story, but having a bedtime routine that is soothing and consistent will help you to sleep. Blue light is also associated with sleep problems. Turn off your phone and laptop as part of your sleep routine. Reading a book or listening to quiet music can help you to drift off to sleep.
- Make sure where you sleep is as quiet and dark as possible. Purchase earplugs and a sleep mask if needed.
- Get outside during the day. Sunlight helps release melatonin at bedtime and also sets circadian rhythms.

Source: Burrell, 2013.

block of reading time. If you are studying and find yourself losing concentration at times, give yourself an LC, for "losing concentration." If you start to do some homework problems and find yourself getting so distracted that you don't accomplish any work, or if the material just seems more difficult than it should, give yourself a D, for "distracted" or "difficult." These are just examples. The idea is to see whether a pattern emerges as to when you concentrate, think, and remember best. You might also see that after a night of almost no sleep, you are "brain dead" most of the next day.

Naps and Wakeful Rest

Did you know that humans are supposed to nap every afternoon? It's true. William C. Dement, founder of the Stanford University Sleep Clinic and the father of sleep research, found that the human brain experiences transient sleepiness in the midafternoon and that there is nothing we can do about it. In fact, Dement says humans function best with a good night's rest and a short afternoon nap. A person's desire to nap in midafternoon varies in degree, but the fact remains that our brains do not function very well when they want to be asleep (Dement & Vaughan, 1999). Psychologist James Maas points out that naps "greatly strengthen the ability to pay close attention to details and to make critical decisions." He adds that "naps taken about 8 hours after you wake have been proven to do much more for you than if you added those 20 or 30 minutes onto your night time sleep" (Maas & Robbins, 2011, p. 33).

The latest evidence about naps is that the best nap is one that lasts 90 minutes (Loeb, 2015). This is because you will complete an entire sleep cycle going through all five stages of sleep and be more likely to wake easily feeling rested. Naps that last 20 minutes are also helpful as they allow you to wake before you get into a deep state of sleep. The key is to nap for about 20 minutes or about 90 minutes. Naps in the range of 45 to 75 minutes, particularly when alarms are set, may cause you to wake up when your brain is in the deep state of sleep, which may make you feel very groggy and render you unable to function effectively for some time after awakening. Individuals who say they dislike napping because it makes them feel worse may well be sleeping for about 60 minutes and using an alarm to wake up.

The elite soccer teams in Europe all have sleep coaches who require their players to take a 90-minute nap each day. The naps improved player performance in afternoon practices. These coaches also work with the players to develop sleep habits that help them to get an excellent night's rest before a game, enhancing their performance (Hall, 2017).

Another excellent way to consolidate memories, especially if you have afternoon classes, is to take a brief nap of 20 minutes. During this short nap, new learning becomes more stable. Thus, it will more likely be available in its original form when you go to practice it in the future.

Researchers at the University of Lubeck in Germany conducted a study that demonstrated that students who napped after learning 15 pairs of cards with animals on them remembered 85% of the cards, whereas students who learned the same cards but did not nap recalled only 60% (Diekelmann, Büchel, Born, & Rasch, 2011). In another nap study, the National Aeronautics and Space Administration (NASA) found that pilots who took a 26-minute nap increased their flying performance by 34% over their performances when no rest was taken. NASA also discovered that a nap gave astronauts a boost in their cognitive (thinking) performance for 6 hours following the nap (NASA, 2005).

One of the dilemmas we all face is that new memories (information just learned) are stored temporarily in a region of the brain called the hippocampus. While in this area, newly learned information is fragile and can be easily changed or forgotten. The information needs to be transferred to more permanent storage areas in the brain or else it is susceptible to being replaced by other new learning. Michaela Dewar and her colleagues, in a study published in *Psychological Science*, wrote that when a nap is not possible, memory can be boosted by taking a brief wakeful rest after learning something that was verbally new (Dewar, Alber, Butler, Cowan, & Della Sala, 2012). Their findings suggest that the point at which we experience new information is fragile and more practice is needed for us to recall the information at a later time. Researchers believe the new input (learning) crowds out recently acquired information, suggesting that the process of consolidating memories takes more time than was once thought. Dewar's work demonstrates that activities we engage in for the first few minutes after learning new information really affect how well we remember this information. Engaging in periods of wakeful rest, including daydreaming or thinking about nonacademic topics, following new learning will help you to remember the information later. The key aspects of this pause are to keep the eyes closed and to not be distracted or receive new information (Dewar et al., 2012).

The findings of Dewar and colleagues suggest, from a learning perspective, that taking classes back-to-back may not be a great idea. Back-to-back class schedules may cut down on travel time to and from campus and allow for better work schedules, but they leave no time for consolidation in the brain of the material presented during the previous class.

Remembering What Is Important During Sleep

Although sleep is an important component of learning, the importance of the material to be learned also impacts learning. According to a study published in the *Journal of Neuroscience* by Ines Wilhelm and colleagues (2011), people remember information better after a good night's sleep when they know it will be useful in the future. This finding suggests that the brain evaluates memories during sleep and preferentially retains those that are most likely to be important and needed relatively soon (Wilhelm et al., 2011). The study also found that the students who slept right after learning new material and who knew they were going to be tested on that material had substantially improved memory recall over students who knew they would not be tested on the newly learned material. The authors suggest that the brain's prefrontal cortex "tags" (p. 1563) memories deemed relevant while awake and that the hippocampus consolidates these memories during sleep.

Sleep Deprivation Impairs Learning and Memory

If you are between the ages of 15 and 25, you are part of a generation that seems to love stimulating their brains with multiple and constant sensory inputs. Whether it is listening to music, texting, phoning, watching TV, or playing video games, you are engaging in activities that can exhaust your brain and impede learning, and you may not even be aware that your brain is tired (Berman, Jonides, & Kaplan, 2008). The problem is that the human brain is not built for constant sensory stimulation.

Constantly taxing your brain is not the only way to exhaust it. Another common cause of brain exhaustion is sleep deprivation. One of the most significant findings from sleep researchers is the profound effect of getting too little sleep on learning and memory. A recent University of Cincinnati study showed that only 24% of college students report getting adequate sleep, and a Brown University study showed that only 11% of college students are getting enough sleep (Peek, 2012). Researchers at the University of California–San Francisco discovered that some people have a gene that enables them to do well on 6 hours of sleep a night. But the gene is very rare and appears in less than 0.03% of the population. For the other 99.7% of us, 6 hours doesn't come close to cutting it (He et al., 2009).

Sleep debt is the difference between the amount of sleep a person should be getting and the amount they actually get. A sleep deficit grows every time we skim some extra minutes off our nightly slumber. William Dement says that people accumulate sleep debt without realizing it and that operating with a sleep debt is terrible for learning (Dement & Vaughan, 1999). The short-term effects of sleep deprivation from even one day of diminished sleep include irritability, impaired judgment, paying more attention to negative information, weakening immune system, anxiety, lower sex drive, worsened vision, impaired driving, and trouble learning and remembering. Sleep deprivation is responsible for one death in a car crash every hour of every day. There are more deaths from sleep-related accidents than all alcohol and drug-related accidents combined (Walker, 2017). Long-term effects have severe health implications, including obesity, insulin resistance, and heart disease.

Unfortunately, we are not good at perceiving the detrimental effects of sleep deprivation. Researchers at the University of Pennsylvania restricted volunteers to less than 6 hours of sleep per night for 2 weeks. The volunteers in the study reported only a small increase in sleepiness and thought they were functioning at a normal level. However, testing showed that their scores on cognitive tests were lower and reaction times continued to decline across the 2 weeks. By the end of the 2-week test, these study participants who were sleeping 6 hours per night were as impaired as participants who had not slept for 2 days (van Dongen, Maislin, Mullington, & Dinges, 2010).

In a 2012 study, UCLA professor of psychiatry Andrew J. Fuligni and colleagues reported that sacrificing sleep for extra study time, whether cramming for a test or plowing through a pile of homework, is counterproductive. Regardless of how much a student studies each day on average, if that student sacrifices sleep time to study more than usual, he or she is likely to have more academic problems, not fewer, the following day ("Cramming," 2012).

Four Common Causes of Poor Sleep

From time to time we all face the obvious causes of sleep deprivation: staying up too late because of doing homework, studying for a test, gaming, watching television, texting, watching a movie, or socializing. There are many reasons you may not be getting enough sleep. That said, sleep deprivation may not be from the *quantity* of sleep, but rather the *quality* of sleep. The following sections note four of the most common causes of poor quality sleep.

Lights at Night

Gooley and colleagues (2011) wrote in the *Journal of Clinical Endocrinology and Metabolism* that chronically exposing oneself to electrical lighting (just 1 hour of normal household light after darkness has set in) and the blue light that comes from all of our iPads, computers, phones, and televisions in the late evening decreases melatonin production. Melatonin is the hormone that makes us sleepy each night. According to the Centers for Disease Control (CDC, 2016) one in three Americans suffers from some form of sleep problem. This new finding of the effect of light on our sleep may explain some of these sleep problems, particularly because computer games, e-readers, and television watching has become a common activity just before going to bed. These all produce blue light, which reduces melatonin production and disrupts sleep onset. The good news is that eyeglass lens makers have been able to develop lenses that block 99.5% of all blue light. So the next time you get new glasses ask for lenses that block blue light. If you don't wear glasses, one of the most popular options right now is an app called f.lux, which tweaks the color of your computer's display according to the time of day by changing the intense blue light that makes it easier to read your display in the daytime to a warmer red light at night. It's completely free and you can use it on Windows, Mac, Linux, and some iOS devices. There's an app called Twilight on Android that performs the same light change from blue to red. It may also be helpful to turn down your regular house lighting after dark, especially any fluorescent lights that use blue spectrum lighting.

Alcohol Consumption

You may think alcohol relaxes you and helps you to fall asleep. It is true that it will cause you to become sedated and fall asleep, but the sleep you are getting is not the natural sleep that refreshes you. Rather, it is sleep that is affected by numerous interruptions and devoid of REM cycles, leaving you to awake tired and less able to learn new things.

The evidence regarding alcohol's harmful effects on sleep as well as memory formation and retention is so strong that the only advice we can give you is to abstain from drinking more than one ounce of alcohol when you need a good night of sleep. The average person's body can metabolize alcohol at a rate of 0.16 ounces per hour (Ramchandani, 2001). This means that if you drink enough to have a blood alcohol level of 0.08 (the legal limit to drive in many states) at 10:00 p.m. it may take your body until 4:00 a.m. to have that alcohol out of your system (Doyle, 2017).

Alcohol also disrupts your REM sleep. When we drink even small-to-moderate amounts in the afternoon or evening our bodies begin immediately to metabolize the alcohol and in doing so produce chemicals (aldehydes and ketones) that block the brain's ability to generate REM sleep. As mentioned earlier, the function of REM sleep is to aid in memory integration and association. By disrupting REM sleep, alcohol can cause new learning, which you may have mastered even at the 90% level, to be lost to such a great extent (40%–50% loss of recall) that all your effort in learning it was basically wasted. This was found to be true even when the alcohol consumption came three days after the mastery of the learning (Walker, 2017).

Caffeine Intake

The National Sleep Foundation has labeled caffeine as the most popular drug in the world. It is the second-most traded commodity in the world next to oil. Caffeine is found naturally in over 60 plants, including the coffee bean, tea leaf, kola nut, and cacao pod. People all over the world consume caffeine on a daily basis, most frequently in coffee, tea, cocoa, chocolate, soft drinks, and drugs.

Caffeine is a stimulant. People use it to wake up more quickly in the morning and to remain alert during the day. There is no nutritional need for caffeine in the diet. Moderate caffeine intake, however, is not associated with any recognized health risk. It is important to note that although caffeine cannot replace sleep, it can temporarily make us feel more alert by blocking the sleep-inducing neurochemical adenosine and increasing the production of adrenaline.

Caffeine enters the bloodstream through the stomach and small intestine and can have a stimulating effect as soon as 15 minutes after it is consumed. Once in the body, caffeine will persist for several hours; it takes about 6 hours for one-half of the caffeine to be eliminated (National Sleep Foundation, 2016a).

A big downside of caffeine is that it can keep you from falling asleep at night, decreasing the length of time you sleep. It also increases the number of times you wake up during the night, impeding deep sleep and making your night very restless. The next day you are more tired because of reduced and poor-quality sleep. To feel more energetic and fight the tiredness, you reach for morning coffee. The cycle continues. The key is to avoid caffeine and caffeinated beverages 6 to 8 hours before bedtime ("Caffeine," n.d.). Just a note for you coffee drinkers: Even decaffeinated coffee has 15% to 30% of the caffeine of regular coffee so it can keep you awake as well. Researchers are also looking into reports of seizures being linked to the very high doses of caffeine found in popular energy drinks (Iyadurai & Chung, 2007). Caution should be taken when ingesting multiple energy drinks, particularly when consumed with coffee.

Diet

A less than healthy diet, especially one high in saturated fat, can have a negative impact on the length and quality of your sleep (St-Onge, Roberts, Shechter, & Choudhury, 2016). In a 2013 study, Michael Grandner and his colleagues from the University of Pennsylvania Center for Sleep and Circadian Neurobiology found that people who have a healthy diet and eat a large variety of foods have the healthiest sleep patterns (Lynn, 2013). Numerous studies link sleep deprivation with obesity, so it may not be surprising that a healthy diet is a major predictor of good sleep habits.

Fixing a Sleep Debt

Recovering from one or two nights' sleep deprivation is accomplished by getting a good night's rest. Just one night of recovery sleep can reverse the adverse effects of total sleep deprivation. Recovery sleep is more efficient than normal sleep. Most people fall asleep faster than normal and have increased amounts of deep and REM sleep. A good practice during recovery sleep is to sleep until you wake up on your own—don't set an alarm.

Recovering from a longer period of sleep deprivation can be trickier. First, you must realize that you are the one who decides how much sleep you get, as you manage the demands on yourself and your time. College offers many opportunities, but each opportunity comes at a cost of time. For those who have so many obligations that they sleep less than typically recommended and are coping with long-term sleep debt, the American Academy of Sleep Medicine recommends three short-term solutions for reducing the effects of sleep deprivation. Note, however, that following these suggestions may not restore alertness and performance to fully rested levels (Widmar, 2003).

1. *Caffeine.* This stimulant can provide improved alertness and performance at doses of 75 mg to 150 mg after acute sleep loss. Higher doses are needed to produce a benefit after a night of total sleep loss. A person who uses caffeine frequently can build up a tolerance, which makes it less and less effective. Caffeine, although helpful when you are sleep deprived but must function, as mentioned previously, also interferes with getting restful sleep. Sleep scientists recommend stopping caffeine intake 6 hours before bedtime.

2. *Naps.* During a period of sleep loss, a brief nap of 20 minutes or less or a 90-minute nap may boost alertness. Be cautious of naps in between these times, because they can be challenging to wake up from, and they may also produce severe grogginess, or sleep inertia, that persists after waking up.

3. *Doctor visit.* Talk to your doctor about why you are failing to get adequate sleep and ask for recommendations for coping with the sleep debt.

The following are some additional tips for getting and staying out of sleep debt (Smith, Robinson, & Segal, 2013):

• *Schedule time for sleep and aim for at least 7.5 hours of sleep every night.* Block off enough time for sleep each night so that you don't fall further in debt. It may be helpful to keep a sleep diary in which you record when you go to bed, when you get up, your total hours of sleep, and how you feel throughout the day. As you keep track of your sleep, you'll discover your natural patterns and get to know your sleep needs. Consistency is the key.

- *Settle short-term sleep debt as soon as possible.* Recovery sleep can quickly get you back to optimum learning levels.
- *Pay attention to what you eat and drink.* Don't go to bed hungry or stuffed. The discomfort you will experience might keep you up. Also avoid a high-fat diet as it has been shown to disrupt sleep (St-Onge et al., 2016).
- *Nicotine, caffeine, and alcohol deserve caution, too.* The stimulating effects of nicotine and caffeine, which take hours to wear off, can wreak havoc on quality sleep. And even though alcohol might make you feel sleepy, it disrupts sleep later in the night.
- *Create a bedtime ritual.* Do the same things each night to tell your body it's time to wind down. This routine might include taking a warm bath or shower, reading a book, or listening to soothing music with the lights dimmed.
- *Get comfortable.* Create a room that's ideal for sleeping. Often this means cool, dark, and quiet. Room temperatures between 60 and 67 degrees are ideal for promoting sleep.
- *Limit daytime naps.* Long daytime naps can interfere with nighttime sleep, especially if you're struggling with insomnia or poor sleep quality at night. Naps can be very positive but should be limited to one nap of 20 minutes or 90 minutes. It is best to take naps approximately 8 hours after you wake up in the morning.
- *Include physical activity in your daily routine.* Regular physical activity can promote better sleep, helping you to fall asleep faster and to enjoy deeper sleep. However, if you exercise too close to bedtime, you might be too energized to fall asleep.
- *Avoid bright lights and blue light from phones, computers, televisions, and house lighting.* Later in the evening these lights can delay melatonin release, which is needed to fall asleep.

Nearly everyone has an occasional sleepless night, but if you frequently have trouble sleeping, or if you are very concerned about your lack of sleep, contact your doctor.

Managing Stress Can Improve Sleep

If you are lying in bed and your mind is racing through all you have to do the next day (a common occurrence when under stress), your sleep is likely to suffer. To help restore peace to your life, consider healthy ways to manage stress. Start with the basics, such as getting organized, setting priorities, and delegating tasks. Give yourself permission to take a break when you need one. Exercise will aid in reducing stress and help you to relax.

In a 2011 issue of *Time* magazine, the Marconi Union's song "Weightless" (Talbot, Crossley, & Meadows, 2016), which lasts a little over 8 minutes, was listed as a breakthrough in helping people fall asleep. A listener's body rhythms will sync with the song, slowing heart rate by 35% and reducing anxiety by 65%. Scientists believe that this song works so well that they recommend not listening to it while driving.

Long-Term Brain Health and Sleep

A 2013 article in *Science* titled "Sleep Drives Metabolite Clearance From the Adult Brain" (Xie, Kang, Xu, Chen, Thiyagarajan, O'Donnell, et al., 2013) reported the discovery that the brain has a waste removal mechanism, which they called the glymphatic system. The glymphatic system relies on cerebrospinal fluid (CSF) to flush out neurotoxins (these are the byproducts of the brain's electrical and chemical activities that take place all day long) via pathways separate from the rest of the body's waste removal system (lymphatic system). Later in 2013 the research team followed up on this discovery by identifying "hidden caves" that open in the brain while we sleep, allowing cerebrospinal fluid to flush out neurotoxins, safely removing them through the bloodstream. Why is this discovery so important? The answer is that it is these very neurotoxins that are suspected of causing a variety of neurological diseases, including Alzheimer's. Not getting enough sleep over time allows these toxins to build up in the brain. The implications of this research can't be overstated; failing to get enough sleep isn't just a bad idea for all of the reasons we already know, but research is suggesting that over time a lack of sleep may lead to neurological disorders like Alzheimer's—so tell your parents to get some sleep!

Athletes and Sleep

If you are an athlete at any level of a sport, then you know how important caring for your body and mind is to optimize your performance. "Getting enough sleep is crucial for athletic performance," says David Geier (cited in Griffin, 2014, para. 2), an orthopedic surgeon and sports medicine specialist in Charleston, South Carolina. Studies show that good sleep improves speed, accuracy, and reaction time in athletes. When you sleep your brain "practices" the very same motor skills you have been working on during your daytime training or athletic practices. This practice by the brain occurs at a level below consciousness so the skills you are trying to improve become instinctual—you don't have to think about them to do them correctly. You have heard the expression "Practice makes perfect." Sleep facilitates that practice to help you better approach the perfect level of performance. You can literally go to bed struggling to perform a particular skill and wake up being able to do it better. This is the power of sleep.

Lack of Sleep's Effects on Performance

When you get less than 8 hours of sleep, and almost certainly if you get less than 6 hours, the following occurs to your brain and body:

1. Your time to physical exhaustion drops by 10% to 30%.
2. Your aerobic output is significantly reduced—meaning less energy to spend.
3. Limb extension and vertical leap are shortened.
4. Peak and sustained muscle strength are diminished.
5. Your cardiovascular, metabolic, and respiratory capabilities are hampered.
6. You experience faster buildup of lactic acid.
7. Your body's blood oxygen saturation is decreased and carbon dioxide in the blood is increased.
8. You have a lowered ability to sweat and thus cool yourself.

9. You have a greater risk of injury—a 75% increased likelihood after less than 6 hours of sleep (Walker, 2017).

Does Sleep Boost Athletic Achievement?

In preliminary research on swimmers, tennis players, and members of the Stanford football team, a study recently published in the *Journal of Sleep* by Cheri Mah and her colleagues (Mah, Mah, Kezirian, & Dement, 2011) jolted the world of sports analytics by showing that you can get safe, legal human growth hormone (HGH) (produced by your own body) just by shutting off the lights and getting enough sleep. Over three seasons, from 2005 to 2008, Mah and her team studied Stanford basketball team members. For 2 to 4 weeks, the Cardinal players kept to their normal schedules. Then for 5 to 7 weeks, they carefully monitored what they drank, took daytime naps, and tried to sleep 10 hours every night. After increasing their daily rest, the players sprinted faster and said that they felt better in practice and games. Their aim got better as well. Their 3-point shooting jumped by 9.2% and their free throw percentage increased by 9% (Mah et al., 2011).

Research by Van Cauter and Broussard (2016) showed that sleep deprivation (7 or fewer hours a night for most people) after only 1 week caused young, healthy males to have glucose (the energy source for the brain and body) levels that were below normal and also showed a rapid deterioration of the body's functions. This reduced ability of the body to manage glucose was similar to that found in the elderly.

Another finding in Van Cauter and Broussard's research was that increased levels of the stress hormone cortisol occur when we do not get enough sleep. Cortisol is an important and helpful part of the body's response to stress; however, when cortisol levels are too high or too low, negative effects on the body and mind emerge, including impaired cognitive performance, decreases in muscle tissue and bone density, and increased blood pressure. Sleep deprivation has also been shown to lower production of glycogen and carbohydrates that are stored for energy use during physical activity. In short, less sleep increases the possibility of fatigue, low energy, and less focus at game time. It may also slow recovery postgame (Van Cauter & Broussard, 2016).

Sleep plays a major role in athletic performance and impacts competitive results. The quality and amount of sleep athletes get is often the key to winning. REM sleep in particular provides energy to both the brain and body. If sleep is cut short, the body doesn't have time to repair memory, consolidate memories, and release hormones needed for good health (National Sleep Foundation, 2016c). Further, sleeping for long stretches is naturally anabolic: During deep sleep, our bodies release growth hormones, which stimulate the healing and growth of muscle and bone. So although it is possible to get through a day following a lack of sleep, proper sleep helps athletes in two ways. First, it boosts areas of performance that require top-notch cognitive function, like reaction time and hand-eye coordination. Second, it aids recovery from tough games and workouts by increasing the body's ability to reduce inflammation and repair muscles. Sleep allows athletes to restock cellular energy in the form of glucose and glycogen (Keating, 2012). Sleep specialist Mark Rosekind, a former NASA scientist, pushed for Olympians to get 9 to 10 hours of sleep a night, not the 5 to 7 hours most young adults manage. "People need to be as smart about sleep," Rosekind said, "as they are about diet and exercise" (cited in Keating, 2012, para. 5). Jim Thornton, president of the National Athletic Trainers' Association, says athletes in training should sleep about an hour extra per day. To get the extra sleep you can go to sleep earlier or take an afternoon nap (cited in Griffin, 2014). A 2015 study appearing in *Sports Medicine* (Fullagar et al., 2015) showed that a reduction in sleep quality and quantity could result in an autonomic nervous system imbalance, simulating symptoms of the overtraining syndrome. Additionally, increases in proinflammatory cytokines following sleep loss could promote immune system dysfunction and make it easier to get sick. More importantly, many studies investigating the effects of sleep loss on cognitive function report slower and less accurate cognitive performance. The bottom line is sleep has a massive impact on athletic performance at every level. It is difficult when exhausted to read, to study for an exam, and to perform well at a physical activity. In order to play well you need to sleep well—not just for yourself but for the good of your team.

Chapter Summary

Sleep is so vital to the human body and brain that a continued lack of it can lead to severe illnesses and even death. That's why people never try to stay awake for days at a time. What many students do not know is that a full night's sleep every night is vital to learning, forming memories, and being your best at performance-related activities. While sleeping, humans make memories and the human brain clears away unwanted information so that it will be ready to learn the next day. When you are sleep deprived, your ability to pay attention and learn new information is impaired, and your brain has trouble making memories for information that you need to remember, such as your course work. In addition, physical activities, such as sports, are impacted severely by a loss of sleep.

Following are the key ideas from this chapter:

1. Memories are made during sleep.
2. Almost every person needs 7.5 to 9 hours of sleep each night, and teenagers often need 9 to 10 hours.
3. Sleep is when the brain clears the hippocampus of unwanted information so that it is ready to learn new information the next day.
4. Each person has his or her own sleep pattern. Some are early to bed and early to rise, some are night owls, and some fall in between. It is important to identify your sleep pattern.
5. The brain remembers best what is most important to you, and recalling the most important information right before bed improves memory formation for that information.
6. A daily 20-minute nap is great for improving learning and memory, but a nap of 60 minutes will leave you feeling lethargic and potentially in a bad mood.
7. Constant sensory stimulation of your brain (e.g., listening to music hour after hour or constantly texting) can exhaust the brain and make learning difficult.

8. Sleep deprivation is harmful to learning and memory.
9. If you have significant sleep problems, get help immediately. Sleep is vital to college success.
10. Having adequate sleep increases athletic performance at all levels.

Critical Thinking and Discussion Questions

1. How much sleep do you average each night? To what extent do you feel this has an impact on your life? If you are not sleeping enough each night, what changes in your life could you make that would allow you to get at least 7 hours of sleep?
2. Would you consider yourself more of a lark or a night owl? Describe how you feel at different times of the day when you are not sleep deprived. That is, if you are not exhausted, when do you feel the best during the day? In what way can this information determine how to best structure your day?
3. Do you nap regularly? Why or why not? What is a good and poor length of time for a nap? What are the values of napping?
4. What is a sleep debt, how is it caused, and to what extent are people good at recognizing when they are accumulating a sleep debt? What are the consequences of having a sleep debt? How do you feel when you have a sleep debt?
5. What strategies do you use to maximize your sleep, both in terms of amount and quantity?
6. Describe at least three major impacts of sleep on athletic performance.
7. Based on the information in this chapter, describe actions that you can take to improve your learning or athletic performance.

References

American Academy of Sleep Medicine. (2008, May 15). Morningness a predictor of better grades in college [News release]. Retrieved from http://www.aasmnet.org/articles.aspx?id=887

American Association for the Advancement of Science (AAAS). (2011, March 8). *As we sleep, speedy brain waves boost our ability to learn.* Retrieved from https://www.eurekalert.org/pub_releases/2011-03/uoc--aws030211.php

Berman, M., Jonides, J., & Kaplan, S. (2008, December). The cognitive benefits of interacting with nature. *Psychological Science, 19,* 1207–1212.

Beth Israel Deaconess Medical Center. (2005, June 29). Study shows how sleep improves memory [News release]. *Science Daily.* Retrieved from http://www.sciencedaily.com/releases/2005/06/050629070337.htm

Brain's learning ability seems to recharge during light slumber [News release]. (2011, March 8). *Health Day News.* Retrieved from https://consumer.healthday.com/cognitive-health-information-26/brain-health-news-80/brain-s-learning-ability-seems-to-recharge-during-light-slumber-650627.html

Burrell, J. (2013). College kids, sleep and the GPA connection [Web log post]. Retrieved from http://youngadults.about.com/od/healthandsafety/a/Sleep.htm

Buzsáki, G., Girardeau, G., Benchenane, K., Wiener, S., & Zugaro, M. (2009). Selective suppression of hippocampal ripples impairs spatial memory. *Nature Neuroscience, 12,* 1222–1223.

Caffeine. (n.d.). *SleepDisordersGuide.com.* Retrieved from http://www.sleepdisordersguide.com/topics/caffeine.html

Campus Mind Works, University of Minnesota. (2016). *Sleep.* Retrieved from http://campusmindworks.org/students/self_care/sleep.asp

Centers for Disease Control and Prevention (CDC). (2016, February). One in three adults don't get enough sleep [News release]. Retrieved from http://www.cdc.gov/media/releases/2016/p0215-enough-sleep.html

Cramming for a test? Don't do it, say UCLA researchers. (2012, August 22). *UC Health.* Retrieved from http://health.universityofcalifornia.edu/2012/08/22/cramming-for-a-test-dont-do-it-say-ucla-researchers/

Dement, W. (2013). *The sleep well.* Retrieved from http://www.stanford.edu/~dement/

Dement, W. C., & Vaughan, H. C. (1999). *The promise of sleep.* New York, NY: Delacourt Press.

Dewar, M., Alber, J., Butler, C., Cowan, N., & Della Sala, S. (2012, September). Brief wakeful resting boosts new memories over the long term. *Psychological Science, 23*(9), 955–960.

Diekelmann, S., Büchel, C., Born, J., & Rasch, B. (2011, January 23). Labile or stable: Opposing consequences for memory when reactivated during wakefulness and sleep. *Nature Neuroscience, 14,* 381–386.

Doyle, J. (2017, December). *Training for intervention procedures.* Presentation on alcohol use and prevention at Ferris State University, Big Rapids, MI.

Fullagar, H. H., Skorski, S., Duffield, R., Hammes, D., Coutts, A. J., & Meyer, T. (2015, February). Sleep and athletic performance: The effects of sleep loss on exercise performance, and physiological and cognitive responses to exercise. *Sports Medicine, 5*(2), 161–186.

Genes linked to need for sleep. (2011). *The Family GP.* Retrieved from http://www.thefamilygp.com/Genes-linked-to-needing-more-sleep.htm

Gooley, J. J., Chamberlain, K., Smith, K., Khalsa, S., Rajaratnam, S., Reen, E., . . . & Lockley, S. (2011, March). Exposure to room light before bedtime suppresses melatonin onset and shortens melatonin duration in humans. *Journal of Clinical Endocrinology and* Metabolism, *96*(3), E463–E472.

Griffin, M. (2014). Can sleep improve your athletic performance? [Web log post]. *WebMD.* Retrieved from http://www.webmd.com/fitness-exercise/features/sleep-athletic-performance

Grossman, L., Thompson, M., Kluger, J., Park, A., Walsh, B., Suddath, C., . . . & Carbone, N. (2011, November 28). Most relaxing song. *Time Magazine.*

Hall, P. (2017). Meet the man who has helped Cristiano Ronaldo, Thierry Henry and Sergio Aguero sleep. *Sky Sports.* Retrieved from http://www.skysports.com/football/news/11096/11056726/meet-the-man-who-has-helped-cristiano-ronaldo-thierry-henry-and-sergio-aguero-sleep

He, Y., Jones, C. R., Fujiki, N., Xu, Y., Guo, B., Holder, J., . . . & Fu, Y. (2009, August). The transcriptional repressor DEC2 regulates sleep length in mammals. *Science, 325*(5942), 866–870.

Hershner, S., & Chevin, R. D. (2014, June 23). Causes and consequences of sleepiness among college students. *Nature and Science of Sleep 6,* 73–84.

Iyadurai, S. J., & Chung, S. S. (2007, May 10). New-onset seizures in adults: Possible association with consumption of popular energy drinks. *Epilepsy Behavior, 10*(3), 504–508.

Keating, P. (2012). Sleeping giants. *ESPN.* Retrieved from http://www.espn.com/espn/commentary/story/_/id/7765998/for-athletes-sleep-new-magic-pill

Loeb, J. (2015). New student orientation. Presentation at Western Michigan School of Medicine on Sleep and Learning.

Lynn, J. (2013, February 8). New Penn study links eating, sleeping habits. *Newsworks.* Retrieved from http://www.newsworks.org/index.php/local//healthscience/50754

Maas, J., & Robbins, R. (2011). *Sleep for success! Everything you must know about sleep but are too tired to ask.* Bloomington, IN: Authorhouse.

Mah, C., Mah, K. E., Kezirian, E. J., & Dement, W. C. (2011). The effects of sleep extension on the athletic performance of collegiate basketball players. *Sleep, 34*(7), 943–950.

Naps clear the mind, help you learn. (2010, February 21). *Live Science.* Retrieved from http://www.livescience.com/9819-naps-clear-mind-learn.html

National Aeronautics and Space Administration (NASA). (2005, June 3). NASA nap study. *Nasa Naps.* Retrieved from http://science.nasa.gov/science-news/science-at-nasa/2005/03jun_naps

National Sleep Foundation. (2016a). Caffeine and sleep [Web log post]. Retrieved from https://sleepfoundation.org/sleep-topics/caffeine-and-sleep

National Sleep Foundation, (2016c). Sleep Athletic Performance, and Recovery. Retrieved November 3, 2018 from https://www.sleepfoundation.org/sleep-news/sleep-athletic-performance-and-recovery

National Sleep Foundation. (2016b). Teens and sleep [Web log post]. Retrieved from https://sleepfoundation.org/sleep-topics/teens-and-sleep

Natural patterns of sleep. (2007, December 18). *Healthy sleep.* Retrieved from http://healthysleep.med.harvard.edu/healthy/science/what/sleep-patterns-rem-nrem

Office of Communications and Public Liaison, National Institute of Neurological Disorders and Stroke, National Institutes of Health. (2017, March). *Brain basics: Understanding sleep.* Retrieved from https://www.ninds.nih.gov/Disorders/Patient-Caregiver-Education/Understanding-Sleep

Gillen-O'Neel, C., Huynh, V., & Fuligni, A. (2013, January/February). To study or to sleep? The academic costs of extra studying at the expense of sleep. *Child Development, 84*(1), 133–142.

Payne, J. D., Tucker, M. A., Ellenbogen, J. M., Wamsley, E. J., Walker, M. P., Schacter, D. L., & Stickgold, R. (2012). Memory for semantically related and unrelated declarative information: The benefit of sleep, the cost of wake. *PLoS ONE, 7*(3), e33079.

Peek, H. (2012). *Abnormal sleep patterns lead to greater issues.* Retrieved from http://www.thehullabaloo.com/views/article_2825a6ac-1ee4-11e2-ad21-001a4bcf6878.html

Ramchandani V. A. (2001, December). Effect of food and food composition on alcohol elimination rates in healthy men and women. *Journal of Clinical Pharmacology, 41*(12), 1345–1350.

Rodriguez. J. (2017). CDC declares sleep disorders a public health epidemic. Retrieved from https://www.sleepdr.com/the-sleep-blog/cdc-declares-sleep-disorders-a-public-health-epidemic/

Rutgers University. (2009, September 15). Rutgers research: Direct evidence of the role of sleep in memory formation is uncovered [News release].

Retrieved   from   http://news.rutgers.edu/medrel/news-releases/2009/09/
rutgers-research-dir-20090915

Smith, M., Robinson, L., & Segal, R. (2013, January). How much sleep do you need? Sleep cycles and stages, lack of sleep, and how to get the hours you need. *HelpGuide*. Retrieved from http://www.helpguide.org/life/sleeping.htm

St-Onge, M. P., Roberts, A., Shechter, A., & Choudhury, A. R. (2016). Fiber and saturated fat are associated with sleep arousals and slow wave sleep. *Journal of Clinical Sleep Medicine, 12*(1), 19–24.

Stickgold, R. (2015, October). The power of sleep. *Scientific American, 313*(4), 52–57.

Talbot, R., Crossley, J., & Meadows, D. (2016). *Weightless* [Recorded by Marconi Union]. On AM [MP3 file]. London, England: Just Music

Van Cauter, E., & Broussard, J. (2016, October 23). Disturbances of sleep and circadian rhythms: Novel risk factors for obesity. *Current Opinion in Endocrinology Diabetes, and Obesity, 23*(5), 353–359.

van Dongen, H., Maislin, G., Mullington, J., & Dinges, D. (2010). *The cumulative cost of additional wakefulness: Dose-response effects on neurobehavioral functions and sleep physiology from chronic sleep restriction and total sleep deprivation.* Retrieved from http://www.med.upenn.edu/uep/user_documents/dfd16.pdf

Walker, M. (2017). *Why we sleep: The power of sleep and dreams*. New York, NY: Scribner.

Walker, M. (2017, April 8). Sleep is the new status symbol. *New York Times*. Retrieved from https://www.nytimes.com/2017/04/08/fashion/sleep-tips-and-tools.html

Walker, M. P., & Robertson, E. M. (2016). Memory processing: Ripples in the resting brain. *Current Biology, 26*(6), 239–241.

Widmar, R. (2003, June 1). Sleep to survive: How to manage sleep deprivation. *Fire Engineering*. Retrieved from http://www.fireengineering.com/articles/print/volume-156/issue-6/features/sleep-to-survive-how-to-manage-sleep-deprivation.html

Wilhelm, I., Diekelmann, S., Molzow, I., Ayoub, A., Molle, M., & Born, J. (2011). Sleep selectively enhances memory expected to be of future relevance. *Neuroscience, 31*(5), 1563.

Xie, L., Kang, H., Xu, Q., Chen, M., . . . & Nedergaad, M. (2013, October 18). Sleep drives metabolite clearance from adult brain. *Science, 342*(6156), 373–377.

Zee, P., & Turek, F. (2006, September). Sleep and health: Everywhere and in both directions. *Journal Archives of Internal Medicine, 166*, 1686–1688.

3

EXERCISE AND LEARNING

Everyone understands the value of exercise in terms of overall health. What is much less well known is that exercise has been shown time and again to have amazing effects on human learning. Mark Tarnopolsky, a genetic metabolic neurologist at McMasters University, has gone so far as to claim, "If there were a drug that could do for human health what exercise can, it would likely be the most valuable pharmaceutical ever developed" (cited in Oaklander, 2016, para. 7).

Exercise has vast implications throughout your life. Researchers comparing brain exercise games to physical exercise have concluded that "aerobic exercise—not sedentary mental exercise—is the most effective activity researchers have found to ward off age-related cognitive declines and improve working memory" (Bergland, 2017, para. 6). These same researchers predict that "exer-gaming," or combining gaming with exercise, is going to increase significantly in popularity.

Harvard psychiatrist and author John Ratey (2013) has written an entire book on how profoundly exercise impacts human learning. The book, *Spark: The Revolutionary New Science of Exercise and the Brain,* reveals that when humans exercise, specific neurochemicals and proteins, messengers of the brain, are released in greater amounts. These chemicals and proteins improve the ability of humans to take in, process, and remember new information and skills. Ratey's main message is that exercise is the single most important thing a person can do to improve his or her learning. This chapter will introduce you to some of the science behind exercise and suggest ways to integrate it into your academic life.

The Human Brain Was Meant to Move During Learning

The first animals to have a nervous system and potential for movement had a tremendous advantage over, for example, sponges that had to wait brainlessly for dinner to arrive (Liu et al., 2014). Although a great deal of our evolutionary history remains clouded in controversy, one thing anthropologists and paleoanthropologists agree on is that humans were constantly on the move. Anthropologist Richard Wrangham writes that a few hundred thousand years ago, men moved about 6 to 12 miles a day and women moved about half that amount. The human brain developed while in almost constant motion (Medina, 2008). Unfortunately, modern conveniences make it possible to interact within our communities with very little movement. It turns out this is not helpful when it comes to learning.

The Disadvantage of Sitting at Your Desk

An abundance of evidence supports the importance of exercise in students' ability to learn (Bolz, Heigele, & Bischofberger, 2015; Ratey, 2013; Reilly, Buskist, & Gross, 2012). It is quite likely that you are much better off being in motion when trying to think about how to solve a problem, when developing concepts for a paper, or trying to produce a great idea (Ratey, 2013). In some significant ways schools have had it wrong for 200 years. Although sitting at desks is practical for taking notes, it is not nearly as effective as walking about would be to learn the new material. New research strongly suggests sitting for long periods of time (9–11 hours a day) has been shown to be bad for your physical health. Some researchers suggest that inactivity is the biggest hazard for youth today, equivalent to what smoking was to the previous generation (Sifferlin, 2012).

What Happens in Your Brain When You Exercise?

First, it is important to say that any movement is better than no movement when it comes to improving learning. However, the real benefit that neuroscience researchers have discovered comes from regular physical activity/exercise and, in particular, aerobic exercise. Aerobic exercise is an activity that raises the body's demand for oxygen, resulting in a temporary increase in rate of respiration and heart rate. Your heart becomes stronger and works more efficiently with regular aerobic exercise. Many in the exercise field suggest that to do aerobic exercise effectively you need to get your heart rate beating between 60% and 70% of its capacity. The appropriate heart rate level is different for everyone. The formula to figure out what your heart rate should be can be found in Table 3.1. In the table, you can see that if you are 20 years old, your initial 50% target heart rate would be 80 beats per minute. As with any new exercise program you should always check with your doctor before getting started. Knowing your target heart rate can help you pace yourself during aerobic exercise sessions. The heart rate chart gives target heart rates based on percentage of maximum heart rate according to your age.

Aerobic exercise can be any activity that uses large muscles in continuous rhythmic motion to elevate your heart rate (e.g., jogging, bicycling, rowing, swimming). The American Heart Association (AHA) recommends aerobic activity for at least 30 minutes on most days of the week. According to the AHA, your target heart rate should be 50% of your maximum heart rate for the first few weeks. You can build up to 75% gradually over a 6-month period and then up to 85%. These are target values. You don't have to exercise that hard to stay in shape. For the sake of learning and health, you just need to have aerobic exercise in your life (Mayo Clinic, 2013).

TABLE 3.1 Target Heart Rate During Exercise	
Age	Minimum–Maximum Heart Rate (beats per minute)
15	123–164
20	120–160
25	117–156
30	114–152
35	111–148
40	108–144
45	105–140
50	102–136
55	99–132
60	96–128
65	90–120
70	90–120
75	87–116

Source: From Heart rate chart. (2009). www.heart.com/heart-rate-chart.html

How Do We Know That We Should Move to Learn?

Flash forward from 200,000 years ago to 1995. In that year Carl Cotman, director of the Institute for Brain Aging and Dementia at the University of California–Irvine, discovered that exercise sparks the master molecule of the learning process: brain-derived neurotrophic factor (BDNF) (Cotman, Berchtold, & Christie, 2007). BDNF is a protein produced inside nerve cells when they are active. BDNF serves as fertilizer for brain cells, keeping them functioning and growing, as well as spurring the growth of new neurons. BDNF makes learning easier. With this discovery, Cotman demonstrated a direct biological connection between movement and learning. Since Cotman's finding, there have been thousands of studies done on BDNF, showing its power to improve learning.

Ratey (2013) writes, "Exercise strengthens the cellular machinery of learning by creating BDNF which gives synapses the tools they need to take in information, process it, associate, remember it and put it in context" (p. 45). BDNF improves every aspect of the learning process at the cellular level. Ratey calls BDNF "Miracle Gro for the Brain" (p. 45). UCLA neuroscientist Fernando Gómez-Pinilla's research has also noted that a brain low on BDNF shuts itself off to new information (Vaynman, Ying, & Gomez-Pinilla, 2004).

Brain-Derived Neurotrophic Factor

When the protein BDNF is present in your brain in greater amounts, your brain is better able to make the connections among the brain cells (neural networks) that are the physical representation of what you have learned. To reiterate, BDNF actually makes learning easier. The last statement is so important that we are going to say it again—BDNF produced by exercise makes learning easier. BDNF also works to limit the impact of stress on the brain and protect the brain from some diseases (Modie, 2003). If you lack BDNF you actually make it harder to learn.

Exercise Increases Production of Vital Neurochemicals Needed for Learning

Exercise increases the production of three particularly important neurochemicals involved in learning: serotonin, dopamine, and norepinephrine. These three neurochemicals help your brain to be alert, attentive, motivated for learning, and positive toward learning (because they improve mood). They also help to enhance our patience and self-control. All these conditions are crucial to successful learning (Ratey, 2013), but as you know, staying awake, focused, motivated, and positive on a daily basis can be difficult in college. If you are alert, focused, attentive, positive, motivated, and engaged in the learning activities of the class, you likely have found the perfect way to learn. By increasing your levels of these three neurochemicals, exercise gives you the tools you need to make any learning situation highly productive.

Exercise Helps You Grow New Synapses

Synapses are structures that permit a neuron (brain cell) to pass an electrical or chemical signal to another cell, allowing the cells to combine in networks. In this manner, cells communicate with one another. Exercise prepares and encourages nerve cells to bind to one another, and this binding is the cellular basis for learning new information. Exercise stimulates the production of new synapses. This is very significant because it is the number of synapses and their efficiency that underlie superior intelligence (Erickson et al., 2011). Or put simply, exercise makes it easier for you to grow smarter.

One piece of evidence that supports this finding comes from a 1999 study done in the public school in Naperville, Illinois, where aerobic exercise was added to the junior high school curriculum. Results showed significant increases in students' test scores, even for tests on which U.S. schools often ranked well below their world counterparts, such as the Trends in International Mathematics and Science Study (TIMSS) test. The eighth-grade students in Naperville finished first in the world in science, just ahead of Singapore, and sixth in math, only trailing Singapore, South Korea, Taiwan, Hong Kong, and Japan (Ratey, 2013). Yes, these were middle-class youngsters from a good school system, but in the years before the exercise requirement was added, the Naperville schools did not match neighboring schools in per-pupil funding or average ACT score. There was nothing to suggest that this kind of accomplishment was in the Naperville students' future. Only 7% of U.S. students even score in the top tier of the TIMSS test.

An additional positive, albeit unexpected, finding from the study showed a 66% decline in behavior problems and suspensions following the introduction of aerobic activities at the school. This improvement in behavior was correlated with the added amounts of the neurochemicals of serotonin, dopamine, and norepinephrine, which have been shown to improve self-control, mood, motivation, and concentration in learners.

Exercise Causes Humans to Grow New Brain Cells

Exercise also enhances the creation of new brain cells. These cells first develop as stem cells and form in the hippocampus, a critical memory area of the brain. The relationship between growing new brain cells and improved learning continues to be studied, but there are indications that growing more brain cells helps improve learning and memory. In a 2007 study, Columbia University Medical Center neurologist Scott Small and Salk Institute neurobiologist Fred Gage found that the new neurons created by exercise cropped up in only one place—the dentate gyrus of the hippocampus, an area that controls learning and memory. The study found that exercise seems to restore the dentate gyrus of the hippocampus to a healthier, "younger" state. Although evidence suggests there is less neurogenesis (i.e., new brain cell growth) as we age, exercise has been shown to be very powerful in keeping brain functions healthy and productive at all ages (Ratey, 2013).

How Much, What Kind of Exercise, and When

The question of how much exercise is needed to experience the learning benefits described previously has not been fully answered. One thing that is clear, however, is that trying to learn something that is cognitively difficult or complex while engaged in aerobic activity is a bad idea. When engaged in aerobic activity blood flows away from the prefrontal cortex (the CEO of our brains) and hampers learning (Ratey, 2013). However, once your exercise is completed, blood flow returns to the prefrontal cortex almost immediately and we now have an ideal time for learning to take place.

In *Spark: The Revolutionary New Science of Exercise and the Brain,* author John Ratey (2013) writes about a Japanese study that found 30 minutes of aerobic activity 2 to 3 times a week for 12 weeks improved executive brain function, which is a key in learning. There is still no agreed-upon number of days per week, but Ratey suggests in *Spark* that 30 minutes 4 to 5 times a week is a good baseline. However, always take at least 1 day off each week.

Learning how to do a new physical skill while doing an aerobic activity is good for the brain and learning. Learning an action, especially complex skills like dance moves or martial arts while doing aerobic exercise, creates more synapses, healthier neurons, and better connections between neurons throughout the whole brain. "While aerobic exercise elevates neurotransmitters, creates blood vessels that pipe in growth factors (BDNF) and spawn new cells, complex activities put all that material to use by strengthening and expanding neuron networks" (Ratey, 2013, p. 55). The more complex the movements, the more complex the synaptic connections, which is very good for learning. Even though you create these new connections through exercise, they can be recruited by the brain for other areas and used for thinking. This process of adapting existing synaptic connections for different purposes is why learning the piano has been shown to make learning math easier. The brain coopts these mental powers of physical skills and applies them to other learning situations.

Exercise and Memory

For knowledge-based information and thinking, research supports exercising several hours after being exposed to the new material. New findings from van Dongen, Kersten, Wagner, Morris, and Fernandez (2016) suggest an intriguing strategy to boost memory for what you've just learned—hit the gym 4 hours after you have learned something new. Physical exercise after learning improves memory and memory traces, but this new research suggests the best results happen when the exercise is done a few hours later rather than immediately after learning.

In the 2016 study, van Dongen and colleagues tested the effects of a single session of physical exercise after learning on memory consolidation and long-term memory: The first group performed exercise immediately after a learning activity, the second performed exercise 4 hours later, and the control group did not perform any exercise. In this study, the participants in the exercise groups did 35 minutes of high aerobic interval training on an exercise bike. All participants were tested 2 days later to determine how much they remembered, with their brains being imaged via magnetic resonance imaging (MRI) during the memory test. Results indicated those exercising 4 hours after their learning session retained significantly more information 2 days later than those exercising either immediately or not at all. In addition, the MRI brain images showed that the delayed exercise group had more precise representations in the hippocampus, an area important to learning and memory, when an individual answered a question correctly (van Dongen et al., 2016).

Balance Balls and Mini Stationary Bikes

There are many ways to add exercise into your life, even if you can't get to a gym every day. Many schools across the country now have students sitting on balance balls instead of chairs. Balance balls allow the learner greater freedom of movement, including being able to bounce up and down at will. This small amount of movement has been shown to keep the prefrontal cortex (the learning center of our brain) more engaged (Kilbourne, 2009). The extra little bit of movement has also been shown to help with paying attention, which is a critical first step to learning anything.

College campuses are increasingly making use of stationary bikes. A college campus in Houston has placed mini stationary bikes under every computer in the computer lab. Students can sit at a computer and pedal away doing miles of bike work while at the same time writing their papers or doing their homework. At the University of Idaho, a stationary bike has been placed in common areas with a table-top desk design, complete with a place to plug in cellular devices to be charged while peddling. Just down the hall is a station where three students can each sit on stationary bikes that face each other to work on group projects while exercising (Figure 3.1). This kind of moderate movement has been shown to improve learning and memory (Godman, 2014).

There are many ways to add more movement to your learning. Some furniture companies now make treadmill desks that allow for computer work, reading, and writing to be done while walking along at one-half to one mile per hour. Several school districts around the United States have installed standing desks for students, which offer more freedom of movement, as a result of studies showing that sitting is not good for learning or your health.

Figure 3.1. Group work desk at the University of Idaho that promotes exercise while working.

Source: Photo by Todd Zakrajsek.

Walking to Class

One of the simplest ways to add exercise to your life is to walk to class or during breaks from study or after class. If you strapped on a pedometer, you would be surprised how many steps you take each day moving from class to class across the campus. Stay out of elevators. Also, park farther away from campus or on the far side of the parking lot (provided the area is safe for walking); this not only is good for your brain but also may have the additional benefit of reducing dings in your car doors.

Exercise and Athletics

Everyone who has ever played a sport knows exercise plays a crucial role in improving any athletic performance. Being "in shape" underlies all successful athletic performance. But what most athletes don't know is how important aerobic exercise is to their mental readiness to play. As we have discussed in this chapter, exercise improves the brain's abilities in multiple ways. It improves its ability to concentrate for extended periods of time, to make quick decisions, and to solve problems, as well as enhancing motivation and reducing stress. Being better than your opponent in these mental areas is often what leads to winning. The important message of this chapter is that you have control over the level of mental readiness you have both in the classroom and on the fields of play.

Chapter Summary

New research findings clearly show how exercise leads to improved learning and memory. The brain's releasing of certain neurochemicals and proteins during exercise, especially aerobic exercise, can cause the brain to be better prepared and able to learn. It is now also known that humans are supposed to move when learning and that almost all movement is good for learning. Following are the key ideas from this chapter:

1. Exercise is the best thing you can do to improve your learning.
2. Aerobic exercise, especially complex aerobics where you are learning a new skill, 30 minutes a day, 4 to 5 days a week is the gold standard for improving learning.

3. All movement is good for learning; walking to class, sitting on a balance ball instead of a chair, or pedaling minibikes while studying all help learning.

4. BDNF is a protein that is released during exercise and makes it easier for the brain to learn. BDNF has been called "Miracle Gro for the Brain."

5. The neurochemicals serotonin, dopamine, and norephinephrine, which are released in greater amounts during exercise, improve your ability to pay attention, focus, and concentrate, while also enhancing motivation, mood, and self-discipline.

6. Memory is also helped by exercise.

7. Exercising 4 hours following new learning improves recall of the newly learned material.

Critical Thinking and Discussion Questions

1. To what extent do you have the time and opportunity to exercise? When you do exercise, what is your preferred type of physical activity or sport? What changes might you make in your life to give you additional opportunities to increase the amount of exercise in your life?

2. Describe the research pertaining to the type of exercise that facilitates learning and memory.

3. Conduct some campus resource research to determine if there are any stationary bikes, balance balls, or other equipment on campus designed to increase your physical exercise. If none exist, explain which offices might be contacted to check into acquiring these items for the campus.

4. Does your campus encourage students and faculty to walk and to use stairs? This encouragement might be in the form of signs, placement of buildings, and even parking lot location. If you were to encourage the campus to create helpful signage, which office would you contact and what might you propose?

5. What simple message about the impact of exercise on learning and memory might you present to someone who has never heard about

this research? Write out a small persuasive paragraph of 150 to 200 words that illustrates the value of exercise for learning.

References

Bergland, C. (2017, April 25). Cognitive benefits of exercise outshine brain-training games: New research shows that "brain-training" programs fail to boost working memory [Web log post]. *Psychology Today*. Retrieved from https://www.psychologytoday.com/us/blog/the-athletes-way/201704/cognitive-benefits-exercise-outshine-brain-training-games

Bolz. L., Heigele, S., & Bischofberger, J. (2015, November). Running improves pattern separation during novel object recognition. *Brain Plasticity, 1*(1), 129–141.

Cotman, C., Berchtold, W., & Christie, L. A. (2007). Corrigendum: Exercise builds brain health: Key roles of growth factor cascades and inflammation. *Trends in Neurosciences, 30*(10), 489.

Erickson, K., Voss, M., Prakash, R. S., Basak, C., Szabo, A., Chaddock, L., . . . & Kramer, A. F. (2011, February 15). Exercise training increases size of hippocampus and improves memory. *PNAS, 108*(7), 3017–3022.

Godman, H. (2014). Regular exercise changes the brain to improve memory, thinking skills [Web log post]. *Harvard Health Publishing*. Retrieved from http://www.health.harvard.edu/blog/regular-exercise-changes-brain-improve-memory-thinking-skills-201404097110

Kilbourne, J. (2009). *Sharpening the mind through movement: Using exercise balls as chairs in a university class*. Retrieved from www.balldynamics.com/research/a1237990661.pdf

Liu, A., Matthews, J., Menon, L., McIlroy, D., & Brasier, M. (2014, October 22). Haootia quadriformis n. gen., n. sp., interpreted as muscular Cnidarian impression from the Late Ediacaran period (approx. 560 Ma). *Proceedings of the Royal Society B, 2014*. Retrieved from https://www.ncbi.nlm.nih.gov/pmc/articles/PMC4173675/

Mayo Clinic. (2013). *Aerobic exercise: Top 10 reasons to get physical*. Retrieved from http://www.mayoclinic.com/health/aerobic-exercise/EP00002

Medina, J. (2008). *Brain rules: 12 principles for surviving and thriving at work, home and school*. Seattle, WA: Pear Press.

Modie, J. (2003, September 29). "Good" chemical, neurons in brain elevated among exercise addicts [News release]. Retrieved from http://www.sciencedaily.com/releases/2003/09/030929053719.htm

Oaklander, M. (2016, September 12). The new science of exercise. *Time*. Retrieved from http://time.com/4475628/the-new-science-of-exercise/

Ratey, J. (2013). *Spark: The revolutionary new science of exercise and the brain*. New York, NY: Little Brown.

Reilly, E., Buskist, C., & Gross, M. (2012). Movement in the classroom: Boosting brain power, fighting obesity. *Kappa Delta Pi Record*, *48*(2), 62–66.

Sifferlin, A. (2012). *Why prolonged sitting is bad for your health*. Retrieved from http://healthland.time.com/2012/03/28/standing-up-on-the-job-one-way-to-improve-your-health/

van Dongen, E. V., Kersten, I. H. P., Wagner, I. C., Morris, R. G. M., & Fernandez, G. (2016). Physical exercise performed four hours after learning improves memory retention and increases hippocampal pattern similarity during retrieval. *Current Biology*, *26*(13), 1722–1727.

Vaynman, S., Ying, Z., & Gomez-Pinilla, F. (2004). Exercise induces BDNF and synapses to specific hippocampal subfields. *Journal of Neuroscientific Research*, *76*(3), 356–362.

4

USING ALL YOUR SENSES
TO LEARN AND REMEMBER

New Findings About Human Senses

For a long time, scientists studying human senses believed that each sense operated independently. As has been the case with many beliefs about the human brain, new research demonstrates that this belief was in error. New findings show that the human senses work in cooperation with each other and that when two or more senses are used together, learning and memory both get a boost. In their article "Benefits of Multisensory Learning," Ladan Shams and Aaron R. Seitz (2008) write,

> It is likely that the human brain has evolved to develop, learn and operate optimally in multisensory environments. We suggest that training protocols that employ unisensory stimulus regimes [e.g., lectures without interactive elements] do not engage multisensory learning mechanisms and, therefore, might not be optimal for learning. However, multisensory-training protocols can better approximate natural settings and are more effective for learning. (p. 411)

Put simply, a multisensory approach to learning is much better than a unisensory one.

From the earliest teaching guides (Montessori, 1912), educators have embraced a range of multisensory techniques in order to make learning richer and more motivating for learners. *Multisensory* refers to any learning activity that combines two or more sensory strategies to take in or express information (Quality Improvement Agency, 2017). The next time you experience these strategies in courses you are taking, you will better understand why your faculty member has included group discussions, role-playing, or concept map drawings.

Multisensory techniques are not the same thing as learning styles. Multisensory methods combine different sensory inputs. When individuals speak of having a learning style, the belief is that there is a particular sensory mode or modes that best facilitate learning for a given person. We might say a person is a "visual learner," meaning that the individual prefers images, such as illustrations, photos, or a live image, in order for learning to occur. Critical reviews of learning styles have consistently found insufficient evidence that a specific learning style for each learner actually exists, and researchers have shown that trying to teach to specific styles is not an effective approach (Coffield, Moseley, Hall, & Ecclestone, 2004; Pashler, McDaniel, Rohrer, & Bjork, 2008). A letter from 30 leading researchers in psychology and neuroscience from universities in Europe and the United States, such as Harvard, Oxford, Cambridge, and Columbia, noted that teaching to a person's learning style is a neuromyth and that resources would better be placed elsewhere ("No Evidence," 2017). A person who claims to be a visual learner may well prefer visual information over reading, but when presented with a good illustration, essentially all learners benefit.

Even before there was scientific proof that the senses work together, researchers were testing the use of multiple senses in learning. In a study conducted back in 1969, it was demonstrated that students who used both their auditory (hearing) and visual (seeing) senses remembered 20% to 40% more information after two weeks than students who either listened to or read the information (Dale, 1969).

Each of our senses provides additional retrieval cues (ways to recall information from memory) for information and helps build a more accurate representation of a concept or idea. Because multisensory learning gives you more than one way of experiencing something, it's an ideal way to learn. As John Medina (2008) writes in his book *Brain Rules: 12 Principles for Surviving and Thriving at Work, Home, and School*, "Those in multisensory environments always do better than those in unisensory environments. They have more recall with better resolution that lasts longer, evident even 20 *years* later" (p. 208; italics in original). Box 4.1 provides an example of multisensory learning.

BOX 4.1
Learning Using Multiple Senses

During the spring semester, I (T. Doyle) taught a course for students who have ended up on academic probation. I call the class "I Should Have Studied Smarter 100." One thing I want my students to understand is how nutrition affects learning. To enhance recall on this topic, I use a multisensory approach to discuss the amount of sugar and fat in cola and fast-food hamburgers—favorites of many college students.

My tools include a full sugar bowl, a few teaspoons, shortening, and two clear 8-oz glasses. I begin by filling a glass with sugar 1 teaspoon at a time, asking the students to stop me when they think I have put the amount of sugar in a 20-oz cola in the glass. Without fail, they stop me several times before I get to 17 tsp. I hold up the glass so that my students can see how much sugar they take in when they drink a 20-oz cola. The 8-oz glass is nearly one-third full. I don't stop with just this visual display (sensory process 1: vision).

I then pass the glass around the room for students to take a close look at the amount of sugar and to feel its weight (sensory process 2: touch). When the glass is returned to me, I take a teaspoon, fill it with sugar, stick it in my mouth, and swallow it (sensory process 3: taste). Students actually cringe at seeing me do this. I then take another spoon and ask for volunteers to eat a spoonful of sugar.

I want my students to taste the sugar. I can usually get a few helpful volunteers to try it. I point out that we ate only one spoonful and everyone was cringing, yet we will drink 17 tsp over lunch with little thought or concern.

Next, I take out a can of shortening and begin filling another 8-oz glass with 53 g of shortening, the amount of fat in a single fast-food hamburger. I again ask them to tell me when they think I have 53 g (53 g = 0.11699 lb). After arriving at the 53 g, I repeat the same process of passing the glass around the class so that students can feel the weight. When the glass is returned to me, I take out another spoon, fill it with the shortening, and eat it. Absolute horror appears on my students' faces, and no one is willing to follow my lead and eat a spoonful.

Every semester this multisensory lesson on nutrition is identified by most students as what they remember best from the class.

Multisensory Research Findings

In their 2008 study, Shams and Seitz found that multisensory learning increases the probability that the human brain will retain information from a particular event. Their research found that people generally remember little of what they either read or hear (as little as 10%–20%) but that they retain 50% of what they both see and hear (Shams & Seitz, 2008).

A 2003 study looked at learners' recall of correct answers using touch alone, sight alone, and touch and sight combined (Newell, Bulthoff, & Ernst, 2003). The findings show the advantage of a multisensory approach:

Sight and touch   85% correct
Touch only   65% correct
Sight only   72% correct

The following findings are from a 1960s study that compared the recall of information delivered using unisensory methods with the recall of information delivered using multisensory methods (Dale, 1969). The period between presentation of the material and the testing for recall was 2 weeks. Participants either read silently, heard the information from a lecturer, or both heard and saw images that supported the information.

Read only	10% recalled correctly
Heard only	20% recalled correctly
Heard and saw	50% recalled correctly

In a series of studies, Mayer and Anderson (1992) showed that students who took in new information using more than one sensory pathway produced 50% more creative solutions to problems they had been assigned than students using only a unisensory process.

When it comes to learning and remembering, research has shown time and again that combining two or more senses will help you to learn the information and then to recall it at a later time. This can be very helpful when in class or when studying for an exam.

The Power of Smell

Smells are powerful for learning and for making memories. Walk into your old high school gym, science lab, or auditorium, and the smells will frequently transport you back in time. The part of our brain that handles smell, the piriform cortex, is located directly next to the part responsible for memory and emotion (Herz & Engen, 1996). As a result, our memories are intrinsically and strongly linked with odor. To demonstrate the link between odors and memory, Julia Rihm and her colleagues (Rihm, Diekelmann, Born, & Bjorn, 2014) conducted research in which some participants in the study were exposed to an odor while completing a learning task whereas others did not experience the odor. The participants were then given a test over the learning task the next morning. When the odor was presented during sleep, participants remembered significantly more than when the odor was not presented during sleep or a different odor was presented during sleep. The researchers could even identify the effects in participant's brain-wave activity while sleeping.

What does this mean for learning? In using smells as cues to enhance recall, a specific smell can associate directly with what you are learning. Lwin, Morrin, and Krishna (2010) found that after a time delay, scent-enhanced recall of verbal information and scent-based retrieval cues helped in the recall of pictures.

An article in *Science* (Rasch, Buchel, Gais, & Born, 2007) summarized work done at Harvard University where volunteers were exposed to the scent of roses as they slept after studying. The participants in that study were better able to recall the material they had studied, even without being exposed to the rose scent again. The odor of roses, in this case, intensified the transfer of information to the hippocampus, the part of the brain responsible for helping to form long-term memories.

We are still working to understand the relationship among smell, learning, and memory. At this point, we have a lot to learn, but what we do know without question is that odors have a powerful effect on learning and memory.

The Power of Sight: Pictures and Images

Of all of our senses, seeing has the most impact on how we learn. The reason is evolution. When humans were developing hundreds of thousands of years ago, being able to see the animals that could kill them, being able to see the animals they needed to kill for food, being able to see a place of shelter, and being able to see a mate to pass on their genes to were paramount to survival. Paul King (2014), a computational neuroscientist, notes that two-thirds (over 60%) of the brain is "involved" in vision and that about 20% of that 60% is dedicated to "visual-only" functioning. The other 40% comprises combinations such as vision+touch, vision+motor, vision+attention, vision+meaning, or vision+spatial navigation. There is generally a smooth gradation in the brain from areas fully specialized for one thing to areas involved in many things. Any claim to be a visual learner can really be made by anyone who can see—and even by many who are visually impaired.

In a 2006 study by Seitz and his colleagues, student learning was compared between those receiving training in a visual-only mode and those receiving both auditory and visual modes. Findings showed that the students receiving auditory with visual training not only learned significantly more information but also did it in much less time (Seitz, Kim, & Shams, 2006). You can not only benefit from better learning and recall when using a multisensory approach but also learn the material in less time. Taking less time to learn material is something every student should be interested in.

In another study, Najjar (1998) found that students had much better recall of visual information as compared to oral information, and even better recall when the information was presented using both oral and visual methods at the same time rather than just oral methods. Adding images helps to remember information in significant ways. Humans are incredible at remembering pictures. Hear a piece of information, and 3 days later you are likely to remember about 10% of it. Add a picture, and your ability to remember that same information will jump to about 65% (Medina, 2008). From an evolutionary perspective, as previously noted, vision was necessary for early human development. It helped in the crucial areas of survival (Medina, 2008). Hundreds of thousands of years ago, if you didn't see the large tiger hunting you, you probably didn't get to pass on your genes. Biologist James Zull (2002), author of *The Art of Changing the Brain: Enriching the Practice of Teaching by Exploring the Biology of Learning*, writes that "images are by far the easiest thing for the human brain to remember" (p. 145). Translating what you are trying to learn into graphs, charts, or pictures is an excellent way to improve learning and recall.

Concept Maps

Concept maps are visual displays that organize and represent knowledge. Concept maps were developed in 1972 by Joseph Novak of Cornell University. Novak needed a better way to represent children's conceptual understandings of science for a research study he was conducting. What emerged was a visual structure that he referred to as a *concept map*. The value of a concept map is that it allows you to organize and associate information in a hierarchal way and then translate the information from a narrative form into a visual form, creating a multisensory learning process.

A concept map usually includes circles or boxes containing key words representing the concepts, with connections shown by a line linking two concepts (Figure 4.1). Words on the lines, referred to as linking words or linking phrases, specify the relationship between the two concepts linked by the line. A concept is labeled most often in a word, although sometimes symbols, such as + or %, are used, and sometimes more than one word is used (Novak & Canas, 2008).

Figure 4.1. Concept map.

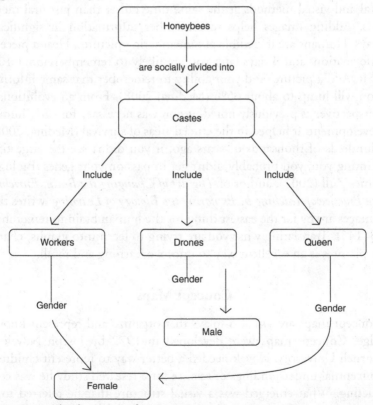

Source: Reprinted with permission from Justin Cooper.

In concept maps, concepts are represented in a hierarchy with the most inclusive, most general concepts at the top of the map and the more specific, less general concepts arranged hierarchically below (Novak & Canas, 2008). Concept maps also contain cross-links—that is, relationships or links between concepts in different segments or domains of the concept map (see Figure 4.2).

Figure 4.2. Cross-links.

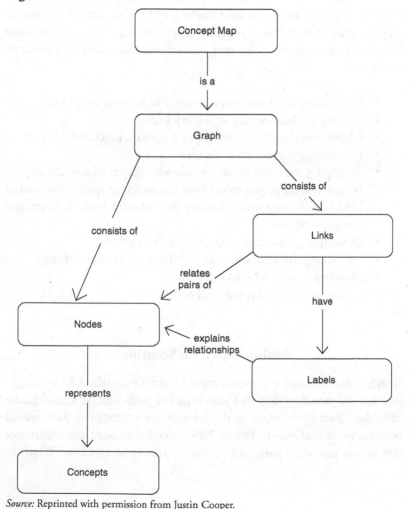

Source: Reprinted with permission from Justin Cooper.

Concept maps are constructed to reflect the organization of a body of information in a visual form. Because vision is the most powerful of our senses, maps are a great way to enhance learning and recall.

Visual displays of information, such as concept maps, are helpful in selecting, organizing, combining, and processing information (McCrudden & Rapp, 2017). Using cognitive maps and other visual displays is very helpful for most students in learning and later remembering course information. This is particularly important for material that you find difficult. The beauty of a concept map is that it has many possible applications that can enhance learning and memory. Following are several examples of a concept map's use:

- Organizing information to be used in solving a problem
- Making a visual display of a story line
- Classifying the characteristics of a person, place, or thing
- Developing a prewriting outline
- Arranging the contents of a textbook chapter in a visual display (which will allow you to see how the entire chapter is connected before beginning your reading and should lead to improved comprehension)
- Developing a persuasive argument for a paper
- Presenting the similarities and differences between things
- Showing cause-and-effect processes
- Creating a visual display of class notes

Multisensory Elaboration

Imagine that you had a home separated from a beautiful lake by a large forest. And imagine that you developed a path that you could take each day from your home to the lake. After a time, the path would become worn and easy to follow. Now imagine that an enormous tree falls across the worn path and blocks your way to the lake. What do you do? You could hire a person with a bulldozer to try to push the tree out of the way—which would likely be quite expensive—or you could take your chainsaw and begin the hard work of cutting up the tree to reopen the path.

This problem could have been prevented altogether had you made several paths from your home to the lake; if one of the paths had become blocked, you would then simply take an alternative path. The multiple-path scenario is analogous to a method for effectively learning and forming memories for your college work. To create multiple paths to important academic information, you should study and recall course information using multiple senses. Studying in this way creates memory pathways for each of the senses. Thus, you will have many paths to the information, and if one is blocked by test anxiety, fatigue, or just plain forgetfulness, another will likely be available.

The process of creating multiple paths to information is called elaboration. Daniel Schacter (2001), former head of the School of Psychology at Harvard and the author of *The Seven Sins of Memory: How the Mind Forgets and Remembers*, writes, "Whether we like it or not our memories are at the mercy of our elaborations" (p. 35). The more ways we can use the information we learn, the more senses we can process it with, the better our chances of recalling it in the future (Schacter, 2001). Using a multisensory approach is one of the best ways to ensure that you can recall information you need when you need it.

The increased understanding of multisensory elaboration is one reason you have been doing more and more group discussions during class times. Although group work and class discussions are disliked by many students, these strategies greatly increase our ability to learn. Researchers have shown time and again that engaged learning strategies enhance overall learning (Freeman et al., 2014; Major, Harris, & Zakrajsek, 2016). The next time you are asked to work in a group, note how different that form of learning feels compared to the lecture, which has fewer overall multisensory elaborative components.

Annotation: A Multisensory Approach to Textbook Reading

Ask teachers what drives them crazy about students, and chances are they will answer, "They don't do their readings." When students are asked which part of college learning they like the least, many give "reading" as the answer. For most individuals, textbooks are hard to read. For most courses, textbooks don't include a story to follow or a mystery to solve. Textbooks for many classes simply list dry facts and definitions. Facts and basic definitions are vital to understanding a subject, but because they are not often fascinating, it can be difficult to maintain focus on and comprehend the material. Reading textbooks can also be difficult because silent reading is a unisensory experience—only our eyes are involved. In addition, reading is a visually heavy process. In fact, reading is the slowest way humans input information into their brains (Dehaene, 2009). One way to make the reading process easier and more effective is to make it multisensory. You can do this by annotating your text while you read (see Figure 4.3).

Annotation is a simple process of making notes in the margin of a textbook that identifies, in your own words, the important concepts, ideas, facts, and details. In 2014 Carol Porter-O'Donnell reported that there are multiple research studies supporting the use of annotation to improve learning. By using your pencil, you add the sense of touch to the reading process, making it multisensory. And there are two additional benefits of annotation. First, by translating what you are reading into your own words, you are identifying whether you understand what you are reading. If you can't translate the material, you don't yet understand it. The process of translation greatly adds to your comprehension and recall of the text material. Second, using your own words is one of the best ways to make remembering what you read easier. Your own words are your most familiar pattern, and using familiar patterns makes learning easier. (The use of patterns in learning and memory will be explored in the next chapter.)

Learning and recall are made significantly easier when you use a multisensory approach. The more senses that are involved, the more memory pathways are created and the more opportunities are available

Figure 4.3. Sample of an annotated textbook page.

Elaborate to Remember

(Daniel Schacter) the former head of the School of Psychology at Harvard wrote a famous book
*called the Seven Sins of Memory. In this book he made the important point that whether we
like it or not remembering something requires elaborating the material. The more ways in   *More*
which you use information the more memory pathways are available to you. If you rewrite your   *ways =*
class notes you form a memory pathway through your sense of touch and sight. If you turn your *More*
vocabulary words into a silly song you make a memory pathway for the song through your   *Availability*
sense of hearing. If you study your math with a pleasant smell present your brain will make a
memory for the math that can be triggered by the smell. [Every way we use our information
presents an opportunity to build a memory pathway for retrieving it. The more pathways the   *= More*
greater likelihood you will be able to recall something when you need it.   *Pathways*

Here is a list of easy ways to elaborate your information.

1. Make it into a song
2. Make note cards and quiz yourself
3. Draw the information into a mind map. This shows the connections and relationships
   between the information.
4. Recode the information. This means put the information into your own words using *use own*
   your own examples—your brain finds your own words easier to understand and recall. *words*
5. Discuss the information with peers in person or online.

Every one of these easy to do practices is an elaboration of the information you are trying to
learn and recall. Each one of them builds additional memory pathways for the information.

Emotions and Memory

In my one of my fall semester 2010 classes I showed my students photographs that were either
of neutral emotional content or were by most human standards highly emotional (a starving   *Emotions*
baby was one picture). I was trying to demonstrate how powerful emotional memory can be for *Powerful*
learning. Spring ahead to spring semester 2012 where I was mentioning to my students this   *memories*
little experiment and one of the students raised his hand and said "that was the starving baby

to recall the information. If at all possible, never try to learn or study
using just one sensory pathway.

Athletes and Multisensory Learning

One advantage athletes have in performing their sports over classroom
learners is that almost all of their learning is multisensory. Most athletic skills are developed by a combination of touch, movement, sight,
and verbal instruction. This very multisensory approach may be one
of the reasons many learners prefer the learning process used in their
sport over classroom learning. As you work to improve in your sport,
take time to notice the different sensory processes you are using to

learn new skills and information. Then take this understanding and apply it to your classroom learning and your homework and study activities. You will find that your ability to learn in the classroom and to study outside of it are greatly improved by doing exactly what you do in your sport practices everyday—multisensory processing.

Chapter Summary

Research has clearly shown that we all learn best from a combination of different senses. Following are the key ideas for this chapter:

1. It is likely that the human brain evolved to develop, learn, and operate optimally in multisensory environments. Because multisensory learning gives you more than one way to relate to new information, it's an ideal way to learn.
2. Those in multisensory environments always learn better than those in unisensory environments. They have more recall with better resolution that lasts longer. Learning is evident even 20 years later.
3. Smell is a powerful aid in learning and memory.
4. Vision is the most powerful of all the human senses. The easiest thing for the human brain to recall is an image.
5. Elaboration leads to improved recall. If you use many sensory pathways, you increase the chances of recalling what you learn.

Critical Thinking and Discussion Questions

1. Describe a situation in which you learned something new through a multisensory approach. Explain the contributions of each of the senses involved. Explain how you could have included another sense or enhanced the use of one of the senses that was involved.
2. Describe a pleasant odor that has a strong association for you. When you smell that odor, what comes to mind? Once you are thinking about that memory, what else comes to mind?
3. Select one chapter from this book, or a reading in one of your classes, and create a concept map. What relationships within the

material emerged and how might this knowledge help you to remember the information at a later time?

4. Annotate a section of reading for one of your classes or the next chapter of this book. When completed, describe the process and what you learned by doing the annotations. Do you feel this approach would help you to learn, and later recall, the information read?

References

Coffield, F., Moseley, D., Hall, E., & Ecclestone, K. (2004). *Learning styles and pedagogy in post-16 learning: A systematic and critical review*. London, UK: Learning and Skills Research Centre.

Dale, E. (1969). *Audio-visual methods in teaching* (rev. ed.). Oak Brook, IL: Dryden Press.

Dehaene, S. (2009). *Reading in the brain*. New York, NY: Penguin.

Freeman, S., Eddy, S. L., McDonough, M., Smith, M. K., Okoroafor, N., Jordt, H., & Wenderoth, M. P. (2014). Active learning increases student performance in science, engineering, and mathematics. *Proceedings of the National Academy of Sciences, 111*(23), 8410–8415.

Herz, R. S., & Engen, T. (1996). Odor memory: Review and analysis. *Psychonomic Bulletin and Review, 3*(3), 300–313.

King, P. (2014). How much of the brain is involved in vision. *Quora*. Retrieved from https://www.quora.com/How-much-of-the-brain-is-involved-with-vision

Lwin, M. O., Morrin, W., & Krishna, A. (2010). Exploring the super additive effects of scent and pictures on verbal recall: An extension of dual coding theory. *Journal of Consumer Psychology, 20*, 317–326.

Major, C. H., Harris, M. S., & Zakrajsek, T. (2016). *Teaching for learning: 101 intentionally designed educational activities to put students on the path to success*. New York, NY: Routledge.

Mayer, R. E., & Anderson, R. B. (1992). The instructive animation: Helping students build connections between words and pictures in multimedia learning. *Journal of Educational Psychology, 84*(4), 444–452.

McCrudden, M. T., & Rapp, R. N. (2017). How visual displays affect cognitive processing. *Educational Psychology Review, 29*(3), 623–639.

Medina, J. (2008). *Brain rules*. Seattle, WA: Pear Press.

Montessori, M. (1912). *The Montessori method*. New York, NY: Frederick A. Stokes.

Najjar, L. J. (1998). Principles of educational multimedia user interface design. *Human Factors, 40*(2), 311–323.

Newell, F., Bulthoff, H. H., & Ernst, M. (2003). Cross-modal perception of actively explored objects. *Proceedings of EuroHaptics,* 291–299. Dublin, Ireland: Trinity College.

No evidence to back idea of learning styles. (2017, March 12). *The Guardian.* Retrieved from https://www.theguardian.com/education/2017/mar/12/no-evidence-to-back-idea-of-learning-styles

Novak, J., & Canas, A. (2008). The theory underlying concept maps and how to construct and use them. *Cmap* (Institute for Human and Machine Cognition). Retrieved from http://cmap.ihmc.us/Publications/Research-Papers/TheoryCmaps/TheoryUnderlyingConceptMaps.htm

Pashler, H., McDaniel, M., Rohrer, D., & Bjork, R. (2008). Learning styles: Concepts and evidence. *Psychological Science in the Public Interest, 9,* 105–119.

Porter-O'Donnell. C. (2014). *Beyond the yellow highlighter: Teaching annotation skills to improve reading comprehension.* Retrieved from http://www.collegewood.org/ourpages/auto/2014/8/17/63598523/Beyond%20the%20Yellow%20Highlighter.pdf

Quality Improvement Agency. (2017). *Teaching and learning program.* Retrieved from http://learning.gov.wales/docs/learningwales/publications/140801-multi-sensory-learning-en.pdf

Rasch, B., Buchel, C., Gais, S., & Born, J. (2007, March 9). Odor cues during slow wave sleep prompt declarative memory consolidation. *Science, 315*(5817), 1426–1429.

Rihm, J. S., Diekelmann, S., Born, J., & Bjorn, R. (2014). Reactivating memories during sleep by odors: Odor specificity and associated changes in sleep oscillations. *Journal of Cognitive Neuroscience, 26*(8), 1806–1818.

Schacter, D. (2001). *Seven sins of memory: How the mind forgets and remembers.* Boston, MA: Houghton Mifflin.

Seitz, A. R., Kim, R., & Shams, L. (2006). Sound facilitates visual learning. *Current Biology, 16*(14), 1422–1427.

Shams, L., & Seitz, A. (2008). Benefits of multisensory learning. *Trends in Cognitive Science, 12*(11), 411–417.

Zull, J. (2002). *The art of changing the brain.* Sterling, VA: Stylus.

5

PATTERNS IN LEARNING

Harvard psychiatrist John Ratey (2001), in his book *A User's Guide to the Brain: Perception, Attention, and the Four Theaters of the Brain*, describes the human brain as a pattern seeking device. He writes, "The brain works by relating whole concepts to one another and looks for similarities, differences and relationships between them" (p. 5). One way to enhance learning of new material is to use patterns that are already familiar to you.

Let's do a simple demonstration. If you were asked to learn a series of 10 numbers—for example,

2 3 1 7 9 6 4 5 6 0

would you find it easier to memorize this unrelated string, or would you find it easier to memorize them if they are grouped into the following patterns:

(231) 796-4560
2,317,964,560

We have asked more than 2,000 students this question; essentially all of them have indicated that the 10 numbers are much easier to recall when inserted into a more familiar pattern, such as a phone number or a big number string. The pattern itself makes it easier to learn and remember the information. You have been using phone numbers and learning big numbers for many years. These familiar patterns give new information greater meaning, which makes it easier to learn and recall.

Here is another example: How difficult would it be for you to learn the following sequence of alternating numbers and letters? They can be recalled in any order:

3 A 1 U 5 I 9 E 7 O

Would this be an easy or difficult string of letters and numbers to learn? Estimate how difficult it would be to recite these letters and numbers one week from today, with no practice. What if we give you the cue of "odd numbers and vowels"? As noted previously, you can recall these letters and numbers in any order. Take a look at the string again. Again, with no practice, most people could recall all of these numbers and letters with no practice:

1, 3, 5, 7, 9 and A, E, I, O, U

Because this sequence fits a pattern you know well, the same task that you thought would be difficult is now easy.

Learning course material is often the same thing. Learning can be difficult or easy with the same amount of effort, depending on the patterns you can identify. The ability to recognize patterns facilitates learning. Changing one's behavior also requires the changing of patterns of responses. Identifying, adapting, and changing patterns are essential aspects of learning. In fact, the pattern of learning is one aspect of higher education that is rarely investigated but perhaps one of the most important patterns that we can explore (Alder, 2010).

Playing Chess

The value of using patterns can be illustrated when learning to play chess. Someone new to chess who learns only the surface rules of the game—the names of the pieces, how each piece moves, and what it means to win the game—will be able to play a game of chess. However, chess is a very mentally demanding game, and having just the basics doesn't adequately allow for appreciating its complexities; novice players with only basic information could not recognize the patterns within the game that would help them decide what moves to make or not make. They can "play," but they can't have a real strategy for getting better because all their cognitive effort is tied up thinking about how each piece moves. Adrian de Groot, the Dutch chess master and psychologist, said great chess players are great because of their knowledge of the patterns of possible chess moves. The more patterns they recognize, the better players they become (de Groot, 1965).

The human thinking process involves actively creating linkages among concepts, skill elements, people, and experiences in order to make meaning by establishing and reworking patterns, relationships, and connections (Ewell, 1997). We use patterns constantly. (See Box 5.1 for an example of how patterns create meaning and make things easier to learn and remember.) Our brain patterns also change constantly. Every time we learn something new, we first try to alter some previously established patterns (assimilation), and if that does not work, we create additional, new patterns (accommodation) (Atherton, 2011). Patterns are so much a part of how our brains work that when we feel like we don't have command of our own fate, our brains often invent patterns that offer a sense of control (Whitson & Galinsky, 2008). For example, if a friend does something unexpected, it takes only seconds for your mind to start thinking up a reason for the behavior. Your brain is trying to determine a pattern to account for the surprising behavior. As you know, even if we are frequently wrong in our assumptions, we can't seem to stop our brains from looking for these types of connections.

Chunking Information

Patterns work so well in learning primarily because they allow you to "chunk" new material—that is, to combine bits of information

---

BOX 5.1
Using Patterns to Make Learning Easier

Note the possible ways to pattern the following words to make them easier to learn and recall:
olives tomatoes bread carrots chicken lettuce cookies ham grapes beef strawberries spinach pork plums mangoes potatoes onions fish duck broccoli cheese cherries brownies turkey

Alphabetical

This is a familiar pattern, but it doesn't help very much:
   Beef, bread, brownies, carrots, cheese, cherries, . . .

A More Meaningful Pattern

Categorizing food words by familiar meals, such as lunch and dinner, gives them more meaning and makes it much easier to recall them. Most everyone would know what is in a salad, a fruit salad, or a dinner entrée. The more connections and the more meaning, the easier it is to learn and recall.

   Lunch: a salad, including lettuce, cheese, tomatoes, olives, carrots, spinach, broccoli, onions, turkey, and ham, with bread, followed by cookies for dessert

   Dinner: a fruit salad with plums, strawberries, mangoes, grapes, and cherries; choices of duck, chicken, beef, fish, or pork, with potatoes; and a brownie for dessert

---

into a cohesive whole. Psychologists noted a long time ago that your brain can process only a certain amount of material at any given time. Amazingly, this limitation is not based on a specific amount of information or material but rather on a number of chunks of material. One of the most cited works in all psychology is about chunking and the idea that the average human can maintain "seven plus or minus two" chunks of information at any given time (Miller, 1956). Although others have argued that we can really hold an even smaller number of chunks of information (Gobet & Clarkson, 2004), the importance of getting information into patterns, which form chunks, remains.

Chunking can greatly increase the amount of information you can process. For example, look at the following letters for just a few seconds, cover the letters, and see how many you can remember:

k s b c e w l o h n

Even if you do get all 10 letters, note the energy needed to do so. Now try this again. Same as last time. Look at the following letters for a few seconds, cover them, and see how many you can recall.

f l a s h l i g h t

Although this list of letters is exactly the same length as the first example (10 letters), it is much easier. Words are meaningful chunks of letters that form a pattern. Of course, this is only easier if you know the word *flashlight*. If you did not know the word, then the single chunk would not be as meaningful and, as a result, not be as easy to recall. Now try the example one last time.

I e n j o y d r i v i n g a l o n g t h e c o a s t w i t h m y f r i e n d s

In this case it is no longer 10 letters that you are remembering, but rather 39 letters. A chunk of information is one meaningful unit of information. One could think of this sentence as 39 letters, 9 words, or 1 sentence. In any case, note how easy it is to remember over 30 letters.

The difference between the three sets of letters is the amount of chunking that can be done. Patterns allow you to find chunks, and chunks allow you to process information much more efficiently. The important thing to keep in mind about learning is that it is not simply the energy you put into the process of learning but your ability to find patterns and meaning within the material you are learning. This is why if you can find patterns in material you are studying, and thus create chunks, it is much easier to learn and to remember.

Familiar Movie Patterns

Following is a list of the 10 most common patterns of modern movies:

1. Horror movie with a psycho killer
2. Buddy cop film
3. Superhero action movie
4. Romance
5. The twist
6. Stereotype shakeup
7. Epic war movie
8. Teen comedy
9. Outrageous comedy
10. The underdog

These established patterns allow you to more easily follow movies and make sense of what is happening. Often you don't even recognize that you have determined the pattern, as this process typically happens automatically. There is a downside to patterns, particularly in movies and stories. If the story follows a pattern too closely, the movie is highly predictable and disappointing. That is because the ending is too easy to figure out. Think about that for a minute. Because it is too easy to figure out, it is predictable and that is not surprising. Directors often alter these patterns within the story line to surprise us—which is where plot twists emerge—and make the film more interesting. However, some patterns are universally followed, and if they are violated, moviegoers are very unhappy. If both partners are killed in a buddy cop movie and the "bad" person escapes, people will be displeased with the movie. The story line would violate the standard underlying pattern of the movie.

In the same way that directors use movie plot patterns, you can use your knowledge of patterns to anticipate what will come next in a class lecture and to help you follow the new information. This will make it easier for you to understand and recall new information. Without familiar patterns, new information is more difficult to follow and understand, and you will need to take more time and apply more effort to find the meaning. Unlike movies, finding the plot and being able to figure out the ending of what you are trying to learn is a good thing. Looking for and finding patterns has a massive impact on learning.

Most Familiar Patterns

What are some of the most familiar patterns to college students? Gestalt psychologists studied patterns in the 1930s and found that some patterns were essentially universal for all individuals (Koffka, 1935). These patterns still hold true today and have been used to help people learn in a wide variety of contexts, such as doctors performing surgery (Dresp-Langley, 2015). Three that are particularly important to learning in school are similarity, figure-ground, and proximity.

Similarity

Look at Figure 5.1. What do you see?

Most individuals report seeing columns of the letter *x* and the letter *o*. It would be just as easy to "see" rows made up of the letters *x* and *o*, but the brain makes patterns of similar items and then makes sense of them by making columns.

In most schools in the United States, teachers capitalize on this inherent sense of similarity and teach students to look for similarities and differences in new material. Being able to recognize similarities can be important to you when you study. If you look for similarities in material, it will be much easier for you to recall the information when it is needed, such as on exam day. Your brain is familiar with the similarity pattern and is accustomed to using it.

Figure 5.1. Similarity example.

X O X O X O

X O X O X O

X O X O X O

X O X O X O

X O X O X O

Think about learning any new concept. It will often be easier if you consider how the new concept is similar to other concepts that you already know. It is easier because the part of the new concept that is similar to your old learning is not entirely new; it's familiar. What you are being asked to learn is just the part that is different from the concepts you already know. The learning task is less difficult when you begin it by using this simple pattern.

The next time you are asked to list three similarities and three differences between two plays know that this task is based on Gestalt laws of perceptual organization, a way of finding similarities that is inherent in the brains of just about everyone in the United States.

Figure-Ground

Another principle that is often used in school is "figure-ground." Your brain, like everyone else's brain, is wired to look for the focal point of patterns. When you look at something, you identify a point on which to focus (figure) and the rest of the image or vision becomes

Figure 5.2. *All Is Vanity,* by Charles Gilbert (1892).

Source: From www.sandlotscience.com/Ambiguous/All_is_Vanity1.htm. ©2013 by SandlotScience.com

the background (ground). If you look at an image, you immediately establish a focal point. In the case of a story, the figure may be the main character and the ground may be the circumstances in which the main character finds him- or herself. For example, what do you see in Figure 5.2? If the "figure" is the woman, then the large light area is seen as a mirror. However, if the "figure" is a skull, the woman's head and its reflection become the eyes.

When you study, determining what is the "figure" and what is "ground" is extremely important. Keep asking yourself, What in this material is most important?

Proximity

Items in our life are separated by time and space. Our brain sees things that are close to one another, either in space or in time, as going together and things that are far apart as distinct. Look at Figure 5.3.

Do you see columns of letters, or do you now see rows? Most people see rows because of proximity. Note that this is the same "pattern" of six letters in each row for five rows as appeared in Figure 5.1. This time that same pattern has different spacing, and so proximity overpowers similarity, and we "see" something different.

As an example, suppose you are having a party and Manuel walks in the door. Then, about 20 minutes later Jessica walks through the door. Your brain would typically not place Manuel and Jessica together. If Devon walks in the door about 5 minutes after Sarah, but Sam arrives only 10 seconds after her, your brain would automatically make the assumption that Sarah and Sam came to the party together and that they came separately from Devon. It does not matter that Devon, Sarah, and Sam may have come to the party together and

Figure 5.3. Proximity example.

XOXOXO

XOXOXO

XOXOXO

XOXOXO

Devon stopped outside to make a phone call. Your brain sees two people coming through the door at the same time and uses this pattern to quickly start constructing meaning.

You establish similar patterns when you process course material. If your history professor talks about George Washington and then shortly afterward talks about the starting of a new nation, your brain will quickly assume that George Washington had something to do with the new country, even if you were not told this explicitly.

In addition, when events happen in close proximity, our brains often infer a cause-and-effect relationship. This assumption makes sense, as causes are often close to their respective outcomes. For example, if you see a person fall down and then seconds later notice a few marbles on the floor, your brain will quickly assume that the marbles caused the person to fall. This is why, when something bad happens, it is not a good idea to be anywhere in the area, as you may well be seen as a cause of the bad thing that happened. People's brains are prewired to assume that those in the near area may be associated with the bad event and maybe even caused it. I (T. Zakrajsek) once witnessed a car accident, pulled over, and quickly went to the first car to be sure the person was okay. He looked at me and immediately said, "Didn't you see the stop sign? You could have killed me!" His natural assumptions based on how things go together made him assume I was involved in the accident. This cause-and-effect relationship determined by proximity is important in learning.

Proximity is another reason that it is a good idea not to schedule classes back-to-back and also to take a short break between study sessions when switching from one course content to another. New information can become confusing if learned close to other new information because your brain will often try to establish patterns, even if none exist. This is particularly true when the subjects are similar, like biochemistry and biology. If you are taking both biochemistry and biology in the same semester, it is recommended to put some space between the class sessions and study sessions for the two courses.

Although similar material learned in close proximity may result in confusion, proximity can also be used to your advantage. If you have complex material to learn, it is important to block off some time during which you can concentrate on that information. If people, a television program, or texts from friends distract you while you are studying, the material will lose its proximity, become less connected, and therefore be harder to learn.

Cause and Effect

What were the causes of the American Civil War, the Vietnam War, or the 1929 stock market crash in the United States? What caused the AIDS epidemic in Africa or the black plague in London? What are the causes of unrest in the Middle East? What effects can be attributed to phenomena such as global climate change or the counterculture movement of the 1960s? What were the effects of the civil rights movement of the 1950s and 1960s, Hurricane Irma in Costa Rica, or the H1N1 flu scare? Students are asked to explore the causes and effects of events as a regular part of their K–12 learning experiences, both in and outside of school. I recall being asked by Sister Mary what caused the fight on the playground in fourth grade (someone hit "Bigs Main" with a snowball). As expected, she looked for the cause by talking to anyone in close proximity to the incident. I (T. Doyle) also recall the effects of fighting in fourth grade, when I had to make 100 snowballs with my bare hands and without my coat or hat on.

Cause-and-effect papers are among the most common assignments in any composition course. It is a pattern teachers use because they know students are familiar with it. More simplistic thinking looks for immediate proximity to explain cause-and-effect relationships. A great deal more thinking is involved in finding relationships that are not obvious by simple patterns of close proximity. In college, students are expected to go beyond basic or surface reasons when finding a cause or explaining an effect. For example, if you were assigned a paper on the causes of AIDS, you would be expected to discuss not only that AIDS may be caused in individuals by sexual contact or blood exchanges but also that the disease is caused by a retrovirus that multiplies in the human immune system's CD4+ T cells and kills vast numbers of the cells it infects (Peckham, Jeffries, Quinn, Newell, & Slowik, 2013).

You might also discuss social implications, such as that the spread of AIDS in children in many parts of Africa is closely related to the health of the mother in the household. Mothers typically protect their daughters from sexual encounters at a young age. When mothers die or are sick, young girls are typically put into sexual situations and AIDS spreads. The pattern of cause and effect, particularly when not obvious, is used to promote deeper exploration of ideas and events that require more critical thinking than sorting information into categories.

Other Patterns Commonly Used for Learning

In addition to similarity, figure-ground, proximity, and cause and effect, most students have spent a great deal of time using other significant organizational structures in their learning.

Hierarchy

In a hierarchy, information is organized in order of importance, from best to worst, biggest to smallest, newest to oldest, and so on. Flowcharts, time lines, outlines, and concept maps are common tools used to illustrate hierarchy to aid learning. Thinking of ways to sort information into categories and then breaking the information in those categories into subcategories often facilitates learning.

Alphabetical Order

From the time you entered preschool, you have been exposed to the pattern of alphabetical order. Just ask anyone whose name begins with an *A* or a *Z*. If you enter "organizing by alphabetical order" into a search engine, you can find websites that will alphabetize material for you at the click of a button. This pattern will not enhance your understanding of the information or show meaningful relationships between pieces of information, but it is so familiar that it may help you to get started when learning new terms or vocabulary words.

Your Own Language

The most important and familiar pattern for you is your own language. The specific ways in which you use, order, personalize, and abbreviate your language create patterns that are easier for you to recognize and recall. If you take definitions that you need to learn and put them into your own language—a process called recoding—or make up your own example to illustrate a concept, you will find that it is much easier to recall the information. Dunlosky and his colleagues (Dunlosky, Rawson, Marsh, Nathan, & Willingham, 2013) investigated 10 different learning strategies and one consistent finding was that anything that required learners to put things into their own words resulted in better learning. Your brain has been recognizing your own language since you began to speak, and the pattern is very familiar.

Suppose you were asked to explain the definition of the word *epiphany*. The dictionary says, "An epiphany is a sudden, intuitive perception of or insight into the reality or essential meaning of something, usually initiated by some simple, homely, or commonplace occurrence or experience" (Dictionary.com, n.d.). It will be much easier to remember this definition if you put it in your own words—for example, "An epiphany is suddenly realizing how something works or what it means and is triggered when you look at or hear something familiar." Your own words are easier to remember, and the act of putting the definition in your own words demonstrates that you understand the meaning. The definition also usually ends up shorter so there is less to recall.

Reading Patterns and Textbooks

Another time to take advantage of patterns in your learning is when you are asked to read textbook material. Textbooks use consistent patterns to display information. For example, almost every textbook has the same format:

Topic
Headings
Subheadings
Paragraphs containing the main idea (which is almost always stated in the first sentence), followed by the details, followed by examples

This pattern holds true for 90% of the text material you will be asked to read. Knowing this pattern means you know exactly where to look for the important information (the main idea and significant details). It also means you know what parts of the paragraph you might be able to skim or skip over (the examples). Examples are only important if you don't understand the main idea or significant details. Otherwise, they can be skipped, which will speed up your reading and help you to stay focused on the important information—the main ideas, significant details, and important examples (the figure, not the ground). It is unfortunate that many teachers tell students that everything in the textbook is important and should be read; this is simply not true. No teacher would read everything. They would focus on just the information they want to know and skip everything else. This is how professionals read everything. Read your textbook with these patterns in mind, and you will save time and be a better reader.

Patterns in Other Kinds of Reading

Almost everything you will be assigned to read in school will have a specific pattern to it. Novels have a common pattern that often looks like the following:

The beginning:

1. Introduces the characters
2. Establishes the situation
3. States the conflict
4. Poses the story question or establishes the situation (which should lead to the premise)

The middle:

1. Progress made as related to important events
2. Characters changing as a result of these events

3. Additional information about characters revealed
4. Events moving toward resolution of the conflict

The end:

1. Occurrence of a pivotal event that resolves the conflict and proves the major point of the story; often called the climax
2. The resolution, which answers the major point of the story, unless the answer is obvious as a result of the climax

Knowing the patterns of a novel can keep you focused and enhances your ability to understand the nuances of the plot. The patterns help you to follow the story and anticipate what will come next, and this leads to improved understanding and better concentration and focus.

With professional journals, as with all written material, there are predictable patterns, but they will vary from subject area to subject area. Researchers have found that learning how to read an article increases both students' ability to complete assigned readings and also their confidence in reading research articles (Sego & Stuart, 2015). The best solution to improving your journal-reading skills is to ask either a librarian or your professor for assistance in understanding how the journal is patterned. Also, ask your professor how he or she reads a journal. When searching for specific findings, many professionals read research journals in the following order: title, abstract, discussion, methods, results, conclusion, and then the introduction. It may vary a bit from person to person, but unless an individual is reading the research journal for fun and general information (yes, people do that), few professionals read journal articles in order from beginning to end.

Patterns in Athletics

If you have any knowledge of hockey, you have heard of Wayne Gretzky and may consider him the greatest hockey player of all time. What many people don't know about him was his unusual ability to see patterns in the play based on how players were positioned and the directions they were skating. One famous quote from Gretzky summarized his ability to see plays unfold: "A good hockey player plays where the puck is. A great hockey player plays where the puck is going to be" (Brainy Quotes, n.d.). By identifying and making sense of patterns during the game he very often was able to be in a position to score or help his teammates score. Recognizing the patterns of the sport you play is a key element to becoming a better player. Point guards, quarterbacks, and soccer forwards do get better through conditioning, but much of the reason some are so much better than the average player at that position is their ability to see patterns unfold. Excellent players can tell by the movements of both their own teammates and their opponents where the open player will likely be. These players are able to do this because they recognize the patterns of movement unfolding before them in real time.

Coaches look for patterns all the time and will often use that information to help win a game. Your coach may have told you that a certain player on the other team always goes to his or her left or conversely can't go to his or her left. You can look for these types of patterns yourself, both in other players and in your own play. This recognition of a predictable pattern can make playing any sport easier. As you become more aware of the patterns of your teammates, your ability to play better is likely to increase. This is not something that is easy to do. Recognizing patterns is a skill that you can build. The good news is that as you become better at recognizing patterns, you will find it easier and easier to spot them. This is why in professional sports coaches and players take a lot of time to watch practices carefully, look at as much film of opponents as possible, and have discussions with expert players and coaches to identify what they have seen as patterns. Coaches also watch game patterns carefully as they unfold during the game. This skill of recognizing patterns can be learned, and it can be enhanced. It is the same kind of skill that works in the classroom, and if you work diligently at this, it will likely make you a better player.

Chapter Summary

The human brain is a pattern-seeking device that tries to connect concepts and ideas to prior knowledge by looking for the similarities and differences between new information and what the learner already knows. Recognizing the power of patterns in learning helps students to improve their comprehension of what they hear, see, and read as well as to recall the information more easily and in less time. Following are the key ideas from this chapter:

1. The human brain evolved to deal with patterns.
2. Patterns are everywhere in our daily life.
3. Recognizing patterns in information is essential to improving understanding and recall.
4. Some of the most common patterns are similarity and difference, proximity, figure-ground, cause and effect, and your own language.
5. Knowing the pattern of the subject you are trying to learn will make it easier for you to follow a lecture, pay attention by anticipating what will come next, and improve your ability to connect ideas and concepts to things you already know.
6. Textbooks are organized into a pattern of heading, subheading, and paragraphs, which contain main ideas, significant details, and examples. The main idea will be the first sentence of the paragraph 90% of the time. Recognizing this defined pattern makes reading easier and faster. If you don't recognize the pattern in what you are being asked to learn or read, ask for help. Knowing the pattern of the material makes learning and recall easier.
7. Patterns exist in every sport and identifying those patterns will help you to be a better athlete.

Critical Thinking and Discussion Questions

1. In his book *A User's Guide to the Brain: Perception, Attention, and the Four Theaters of the Brain*, what does John Ratey (2001) mean when he describes the human brain as a pattern seeking device? Explain an example of a time recently when your brain looked for patterns.
2. Why do you think humans automatically look for patterns? Doesn't scanning for patterns increase complexity and give us even

more to think about? That is, why doesn't this extra work make processing the world around us even more difficult?

3. Chunking with respect to recognizing letters was presented as an example. How does chunking help us to watch movies, read books, and talk to friends? Explain why chunking either does, or does not, require knowledge of the information that is to be chunked?

4. Describe a situation, different from anything presented in this chapter, that illustrates the power of proximity in suggesting a cause-and-effect relationship. When might a causal relationship based on proximity be problematic?

5. If you were to help a struggling student read a chapter in a course textbook, what advice would you have for that student? That is, what have you found to be the most effective way to read academic books, and how does this strategy differ from casual reading of novels?

References

Alder, A. (2010). *Pattern making, pattern breaking: Using past experience and new behaviour in training, education and change management*. Burlington, VT: Ashgate.

Atherton, J. S. (2011). *Learning and teaching: Assimilation and accommodation*. Retrieved from https://web.archive.org/web/20120211191819/ http://www.learningandteaching.info/learning/experience.htm

Brainy Quotes. (n.d.). *Wayne Gretzky quotes*. Retrieved from https://www .brainyquote.com/quotes/wayne_gretzky_383282

de Groot, A. D. (1965). *Thought and choice in chess*. Amsterdam, Netherlands: Noord-Hollandsche Uitgeversmaatschappij.

Dictionary.com (n.d.). *Epiphany*. Retrieved from http://www.dictionary.com/ browse/epiphany?s=t

Dresp-Langley, B. (2015). Principles of perceptual grouping: Implications for image-guided surgery. *Frontiers in Psychology, 6*, 1565.

Dunlosky, J., Rawson, K. A., Marsh, E. J., Nathan, M. J., & Willingham, D. T. (2013). Improving students' learning with effective learning techniques: Promising directions from cognitive and educational psychology. *Psychology in the Public Interest, 14*(1), 4–58.

Ewell, P. T. (1997). *Organizing for learning: A point of entry* (Draft prepared for the AAHE Summer Academy at Snowbird, Utah, National Center for Higher Education Management Systems). Retrieved from http://www.intime.uni.edu/model/learning/learn_summary.html

Gobet, F., & Clarkson, G. (2004). Chunks in memory: Evidence for the magical number four . . . or is it two? *Memory, 12*(6), 732–747.

Koffka, K. (1935). *Principles of Gestalt psychology.* New York, NY: Harcourt Brace.

Miller, G. A. (1956). The magical number seven, plus or minus two: Some limits on our capacity for processing information. *Psychological Review, 63*(2), 81–97.

Peckham, C., Jeffries, D., Quinn, T., Newell, M. L., & Slowik, G. (2013). What is AIDS? *AIDS and Women.* Retrieved from http://ehealthmd.com/library/aidswomen/AID_whatis.html

Ratey, J. (2001). *A user's guide to the brain.* New York, NY: Pantheon.

Sego, S. A., & Stuart, A. E. (2015). Learning to read empirical articles in general psychology. *Teaching of Psychology, 43*(1), 38–42.

Whitson, J. A., & Galinsky, A. (2008, October 3). Lacking control increases illusory pattern perception. *Science, 322*(5898), 115–117.

6

MEMORY

When you sing along to the radio, do you ever think about how you learned the lyrics? Did you practice the lyrics at length? Did you make up flash cards and have a friend quiz you? Did your parents or a teacher make up a test over the song lyrics to see if you knew them well? It is unlikely you learned the songs in any of these traditional academic ways. Most likely, without even thinking about it, you just realized one day that you were singing along—even if you often claimed to others that you hated the song. You learned the song and committed it to memory, without even realizing you were memorizing the lyrics.

Usually, when learning something new, it helps to be interested in it, see a value to it, pay attention to it, associate it with something you already know, and practice it a lot. The human brain is wired to more easily learn things that are important, and for the most part, what's important is also interesting, valuable, related to something you already know, and repeated. So how do we end up learning all these songs we don't want to know? The simple answer is repetition alone can result in learning. It is not the most efficient way to learn, but it certainly will work. You heard the song over and over and over. If you have heard the song many times, then you didn't just learn the lyrics; you overlearned them. A person will overlearn something when he or she is exposed to that thing after it has been learned. Psychologist Hermann Ebbinghaus conducted research pertaining to the impact of overlearning on reducing forgetting that dated back to the beginning of psychology—in the early 1800s. This important concept is still being researched in the twenty-first century, over 100 years later (Rohrer, Taylor, Pashler, Wixted, & Cepeda, 2004). The bottom line is that learning can be done through repetition and that sometimes just learning is not enough. If the information is really important, it can be vital to overlearn the material.

Repetition is important, and by singing along with the song on the radio, you were doing something that is the foundation of repetition: You were retrieving the information from your memory. Our brains are designed to be better at the things we do a lot, and that includes recalling things from memory. To remember what you need to know in school, you need to have repeated exposure to the material and then you need to use it. This strengthens both the memory and the cues for recovering the memory so that you can use the information when you need it a week later on a unit exam, a few months later for the final exam, or even years later in your job.

Another important aspect of learning is using new material over an extended period. You have probably heard on many occasions (and even in earlier chapters of this book) that it is better to spread out your study sessions rather than cram heavily the night before the test. Cramming for an exam is described as massed practice. Distributed practice, in contrast, is repeatedly studying and using material over an extended period, such as days, weeks, and even months. Practicing a list of words for 30 minutes once per day for a week is an example of distributed practice. Studying the list of words for 2 hours straight once is an example of massed practice.

If you are like most students, although you know distributed practice is better, you use cramming to prepare for a test (Blasiman, Dunlosky, & Rawson, 2017). You likely also know very well that feeling of forgetting the material soon after, and sometimes even during, the exam. The reason that material you have studied by cramming is much easier to forget is because the retrieval cues for that material are not well established. They simply have not been practiced enough to convince your brain that the information is important. This is something researchers have demonstrated repeatedly and explains why students who cram for exams may do well on unit exams and then flunk the comprehensive final. Massed and distributed learning are two different concepts, and although massed practice may get you through by a single point on short quizzes or even get you a passing grade on a unit exam, your brain won't end up making any long-term memories for the information.

Each time your brain is exposed to, say, the concept of mitosis in your biology class, your memory for mitosis is strengthened. Every time you retrieve a memory—for example, by explaining mitosis to someone—that memory becomes even stronger and more readily available. The more times you retrieve the memory (particularly over time), the stronger it is ingrained into your long-term memory and the more likely you will be able to remember it when it is needed. Amazingly, retention through repetition is a natural process that you do all of the time without realizing it is happening. This principle allowed you to learn your way around campus, to navigate through your social media feeds, and even to sing the lyrics for a song you don't even like. If you repeat any action enough, it will become a strong memory.

Memory and Sleep

Most researchers now agree that one of the mysteries about how the human brain makes memories has finally been solved. In 2016, researchers figured out that one significant way memories are made is while you sleep. During sleep, memory consolidation takes place when the brain produces new proteins that strengthen the fragile memory traces that develop over the day's new learning (Levy, Levitan, & Susswein, 2016). If these fragile memory traces are disrupted before consolidation happens, learning does not occur. During the active part of your day, when you encounter new information or a new experience, that memory trace can be disrupted by additional learning before consolidation occurs. This is why research suggests you not take classes back-to-back (this is explained in more detail later in the chapter). Taking a break after a class gives the brain time to do some consolidation of new learning. One time at which disruption does not occur is when you are asleep. This explains why a good full night's rest is crucial to the learning process. Sleep is a critical time for consolidation of information learned during the day. It is amazing how disruptive a poor night of sleep can be for individuals and how often we don't even realize it is happening. Try a short experiment: Pay attention to how much you remember from the previous day's learning on days when you have little or poor-quality sleep and still feel tired when you get up in the morning. Compare your recall on tired days to that on days after you've have had a full night of restful sleep. If your findings are similar to most recent research findings, you will notice that you remember a great deal more new information when you have had a full night's sleep than when you have been sleep deprived. Really paying attention to this difference will also help you when making decisions about when to go to sleep and how to get the best quality of sleep. Many college students tell us that they are very busy and don't have time to get a full night of sleep. What is often not realized is that that lack of sleep makes it necessary to spend more time studying because the brain was not able to store the new learning due to a lack of sleep. This is a vicious cycle.

What Happens to New Learning When You Sleep

As we noted in chapter 2 on sleep, sharp wave ripples are responsible for consolidating memories and storing that new information in the neocortex (Buzsáki, Girardeau, Benchenane, Wiener, & Zugaro, 2009). Information stored in the neocortex will be more stable and have a great likelihood, if practiced, to become long-term memories. Buzsáki and his colleagues (2009) also found this movement of information happens primarily when we are asleep.

James Maas and Rebecca Robbins (2011) have noted that sleep has a big impact on memory. Their findings indicate that the final 2 hours of sleep, from hour 5.5 to 7.5 or hour 7 to 9, are crucial for memories to be laid down as stable residents in your brain. During this period in REM sleep, your brain replays scenes from the day and that repetition helps those episodes to become stable in your memory.

Preparation for Next Day's Learning

In addition to consolidating learned material, sleep allows your brain to clear space for new learning to occur the next day. As noted in chapter 2, sleep spindles occur during sleep that network key regions of the brain to clear a path for learning (Walker, 2005). These electrical impulses help to shift memories from the brain's hippocampus—which has limited storage space—to the prefrontal cortex's nearly limitless "hard drive," thus freeing up the hippocampus to take in fresh data (new learning).

Matthew Walker says that sleep is the key to having a brain that is ready to learn ("Naps Clear the Mind," 2010). Bryce Mander, a postdoctoral fellow in psychology at University of California, Berkeley, and lead author of a study on sleep spindles (Mander, Santhanam, Saletin, & Walker, 2011), adds, "A lot of that spindle-rich sleep is occurring the second half of the night, so if you sleep 6 hours or less, you are shortchanging yourself" and impeding your learning (as cited in University of California, Berkeley, 2011, para. 7). Mander goes on to say, "This discovery indicates that we not only need sleep after learning to consolidate what we've memorized, but that we also need it before learning, so that we can recharge and soak up new information the next day" (as cited in Anwar, 2011, para. 12).

Memory and In-Class or Online Behaviors

How you go about learning is called your learning behavior. Significant research points out that learning behaviors have a lot to do with how well you will eventually remember the new learning. The more elaborately you pair new information with things you already know while you are learning, the stronger the memory will be at a later time. When learning something new you want to make it as elaborate as possible. This is done by thinking about the new information in as much detail as possible, using as many senses as possible, and making it as emotional as you can (Squire & Kandel, 2000).

The reason your initial intake of new information is so important in remembering the information is that the neural pathways used to process new learning are the same ones used by the brain to store it (Squire & Kandel, 2000). So the initial moments of learning are crucial to helping us recall what we have learned. Squire and Kandel in their 2000 work *Memory: From Mind to Molecules* explained that the quality of the initial encoding of new learning is the greatest predictor of later learning success for students. So paying attention in class is absolutely crucial to memory formation and recall.

The Impact of Learning on Memory

Another important factor relating to our recall of new learning is recognizing that the physical environment in which we learn something is also a cue to recalling it at a later time. Learning and memory researchers call this context-dependent memory. The more closely you replicate the environment and conditions of the moment new learning occurred, the easier remembering it will be (Grant et al., 1998). A great place to study for a test is in the room where the test will be given. That is often very difficult, so a good alternative is to study a given subject in the same place each time you study. This might be the same place within the library, the same place on campus, or even the same place in your home. Being in that physical place can actually help you to recall the information you learned in that place.

Remembering What We Think Is Important

Your brain will make memories of the information it recognizes as important. Sometimes your brain has to determine what is important. Think about what is likely to be important in your life. Things that we do and say over and over must be important or we wouldn't waste time and energy repeating them. Information needed for survival—for example, asking your loved one, "Did you take your medication today?"—is important, as is information about friends and family.

Material processed when you are excited also tends to be judged important by the brain. After all, if that information was exciting, it must be important to you. This is why an individual will remember the winning shot in a championship basketball game years later.

Given this information, think about the implications of telling yourself that material you are reading for class is boring or not important. If you convince your brain something is not important, while trying to learn or remember the material, you are much less likely to remember or learn the material. After all, thinking about this from the brain's perspective, why use valuable resources to remember something that is not important?

You will also remember what you learn or process just before going to sleep, for two reasons. First, the material is fresh in your mind and other information did not displace or interfere with the material before you drifted off to sleep. In a 2012 study, Jessica Payne and her colleagues found that studying material just before going to sleep created stronger memories for the newly learned information (Payne et al., 2012). Second, think about how often through life you completed a task before going to bed because it was something important. You lock the doors, make sure your pet is inside, set a to-do list for the next day, and say good night to family members. Many individuals train their brains to recognize that things done just before sleep are important. Provided that you are not totally exhausted (or intoxicated), 20 minutes of review right before bed is a great time to go over important information one last time.

Taking Classes Back-to-Back and Memory

Sleep is important for consolidation, but it is not the only time the brain is strengthening connections to information. Researchers Tambini, Ketz, and Davachi (2010) of New York University's Department of Psychology and Center for Neural Science discovered that the parts of the brain that are active during new learning continue to be active up to an hour following the end of that learning. These results demonstrate the importance of postexperience rest (resting after new learning) in creating memories for recent experiences. The brain needs additional time to process the new learning, make important connections, and strengthen the cues to the information just learned. Thus, it is helpful to relax after learning, rather than learn additional information right away. Research has shown that recall of new information was improved in people who were given a break after learning (Schlichting & Preston, 2014).

Overlearning and Recall

As noted in the introduction to this chapter, it is not always enough to learn. Continuing to study and to learn something after you already know it is called overlearning. Overlearning is important for information that will need to be recalled in times of stress or for information that may be needed a long time in the future. A study by Takeo Watanabe, the Fred M. Seed Professor of Cognitive Linguistic and Psychological Sciences at Brown University, and colleagues (Shibata et al., 2017) shows that overlearning prevents new learning or other distractions from interfering with the brain's ability to recall the overlearned information. Overlearning really helps cement the learning into memory.

There is a downside to overlearning. Overlearning may work so well and quickly that for a time, overlearning one task makes it more difficult to learn a second task—as if the brain becomes locked down for the sake of preserving mastery of the first task. This lock-down lasts only a few hours. The underlying mechanism, researchers discovered, appears to be a temporary shift in the balance of two neurotransmitters that control neural flexibility, or "plasticity," in the part of the brain where the learning occurred. "These results suggest that just a short period of overlearning drastically changes a post-learning unstable [learning state] to a hyper-stabilized state that is resilient against, and even disrupts, new learning" (Shibata et al., 2017).

The study shows that overlearning can be a great way to ensure that your brain holds on to the information you need to know and recall. It also shows that if you choose to use overlearning as a study tool you need to leave a few hours as a break between the overlearning activity and trying to learn some new material.

Cramming, Learning, and Distributed Practice

Dozens of studies show it is possible to cram for an exam and do well on that exam (Wheeler, Ewers, & Buonanno, 2003). Studying intensely for an extended period can help the brain to remember a lot of information for a short period. The key part of this statement is "a short period"—typically 18 to 36 hours. Unfortunately, cramming requires a great deal of effort but provides no long-term learning benefits. Research about cramming shows that as little as a day or two following a cram session, you will no longer remember a great deal of the information you studied. Within a week, you will likely have forgotten 75% or more of the material you studied (Krishnan, 2013). You quickly forget the information because your brain did not make any long-term memories for it. For information to become a part of your long-term memory, it has to be practiced many times over an extended period. Practicing over extended periods of time is called distributed practice. Cramming fails to produce long-term learning because the time frame for studying is too short to build the kind of memory that will last.

The practice of cramming also signals to the brain that the information being studied is not important. After you take an exam you've crammed for, you usually have an exhausted, "I am glad that is over" feeling. This feeling tells the brain that the information is no longer needed and can be purged as you sleep. Much of the experiences you have during the day are purged when you sleep, and your brain is very efficient at getting rid of this useless information—things like what you had for lunch, the color of a car that pulled up next to you at the light, or where you parked when you went to the library. Pay attention for just a few minutes later today to how many things you encounter that your brain will purge by the next day. The challenge, again, is to not send the message to your brain that the material you crammed and "dumped" on the test should be part of the purge. Of course, cramming also typically leads to fatigue, and we have already discussed the difficulty of learning when tired. Taken altogether, many factors make cramming a short-term solution without any real positive long-term outcomes. As one group of researchers (Jang, Wixted, Pecher,

Zeelenberg, & Huber, 2012) put it, "If learning is your goal, cramming is an irrational act" (p. 973).

Following is a quick story from my own life (T. Doyle) to illustrate this point: When I was an undergraduate, I took 2 years of Spanish and earned an A in all courses. I also lived in a Spanish-speaking country for a year following college. Yet today I know only about 30 words of Spanish. Why? Because I crammed for all my Spanish exams, and when I lived abroad, I tried my best to find people who spoke English to hang out with. I never engaged in distributed practice with my Spanish, and for all my time, money, and cramming, I got 30 words. If your goal is to learn something that will be available for later use, cramming does not work.

Daily Review Is an Effective Form of Distributed Practice

A good example of distributed practice is daily review or recall of course information. As happened with the song lyrics, if you retrieve from your memory the material you are trying to learn each day, even if it's for only a short period, your brain will make a pathway to that information that is easier and easier to access.

Learning and memory have two key components: the learned object itself and the retrieval cue to find the learned material. Think of it this way: There are many books in the library, and to find a specific book about a specific topic, you look up the call number and then go to where the book is shelved. If the book has been misshelved, the library doesn't have it, or you don't know how to look up the topic, then you can't get to the book. Finding a book in a library is similar to using a retrieval cue to get at a specific memory. Researchers have found that both the memory itself (the book) and the retrieval cue (the call number) are needed for you to remember something.

The best way for you to strengthen both the memory and the cue is to review material on a regular basis over an extended period—a few weeks at least. To make good use of your study time, don't just look over the material or read over the material passively. Instead, try to recall the material. The best form of recall to improve memories are actions that are overt. Saying the information aloud or writing the information down on a piece of paper has been shown to improve recall better than just saying it to yourself silently (Tauber et al., 2017). Each time a memory is recalled, both it and its cue are strengthened, and you can access the desired information in your brain faster. You learn songs by singing them over and over and through the same process of repetition you can learn just about any course material.

Keep in mind that reading (inputting information) is very different from using information through a retrieval process. This is why researchers have been able to show that simply reading course material multiple times is much less effective in building a strong memory process (Dunlosky, Rawson, Marsh, Mitchell, & Willingham, 2013).

Ways to Improve Memory

The great thing about all the research that has been done on human memory is that we now know that there are many proven ways to improve human memory and thus make recall easier and longer lasting.

Familiarity Improves Memory

The more you already know about something, the easier it is to remember it. It is also true that if you know a lot about something, say baseball, it is fairly easy for you to learn something new about the subject. Weiwei Zhang, assistant professor of psychology at the University of California–Riverside, along with colleague Weizhen Xie (Xie & Zhang, 2016), studied how people can learn and remember information when they are already familiar with the subject. He found the more familiar they are with the subject, the faster and better they remember new information related to it. Zhang went on to say, "These results suggest that long-term memory, specifically familiarity, could boost working memory capacity, another example of 'practice makes perfect'" (Feitlinger, 2017, p. 4). Zhang also suggested,

> These findings could have further implications in applied settings such as classroom learning. For example, those preparation courses for MCAT or SAT may have familiarized their students with the testing procedure and the scope of assessments such that the students

could perform better simply because they had better working memory for the testing materials. (quoted in Sherkat, 2016, para. 10)

Exercise Improves Memory

Several recent research studies have shown that exercise significantly improves short-term memory. A study by David Marchant (British Psychological Society, 2016) from Edge Hill University, Lancashire, England, suggests "that an acute bout of aerobic exercise improves your short-term memory" (para. 4). Exercise before learning benefited immediate recall of participants. But when people had to wait to recall the new learning, they performed best when they exercised after learning. "Our findings are consistent with the idea that physical arousal improves memory, and those who need to learn information may benefit from taking part in exercise" (para. 5).

Interest Improves Memory

In a 2012 study at Kansas State University, Richard Harris found that your level of interest in a person is much more important than your natural tendency to remember names (Kansas State University, 2012). If you meet someone and like his or her stories or something else about the person, you are much more likely to remember his or her name. This may explain why some people are so good at remembering names. It is not that that their brains are wired to remember names. It may be because some people are just more socially aware and interested in other people and perhaps relationships with those people. It would make sense that such people are better at remembering names.

Harris says, "Almost everybody has a very good memory for something" (cited in Kansas State University, 2012, para. 5). The key to a good memory is the extent to which the information interests you. The more interest you already have or generate for a topic, the more likely the new information will be learned. If you are reading a topic you enjoy, it seems you won't feel like you are using your memory at all. This is why it seems so easy to learn the things we like and difficult to learn the things we dislike. Finding something to like about a subject you dislike will result in improved learning and memory.

When you are telling yourself a class is boring or difficult, you are actually making it harder on yourself to learn the material.

Elaboration

Daniel Schacter (2001), the former head of the School of Psychology at Harvard, in his book titled *The Seven Sins of Memory: How the Mind Forgets and Remembers*, stressed that whether we like it or not, remembering something requires elaboration of the material. Decorations can be made more elaborate, stories can be made more elaborate, jewelry can be made more elaborate, and information can be made more elaborate. In each of these cases, elaboration has the same effect: more impact. The human brain has about 86 billion neurons, with each neuron being connected to up to 10,000 other neurons. That is an amazing and complex system of connections. When you learn something, the connections formed are called elaborations. The more ways in which you elaborate, or connect information, the more memory pathways are available to you. If you rewrite your class notes, you form a memory pathway through your sense of touch and sight. If you turn your vocabulary words into a silly song, you make a memory pathway for the song through your sense of hearing. If you study your math with a scented candle burning, your brain will make a memory for the math that can be triggered by the candle's smell. If you study both the textbook definition of a word and a definition written in your own words, your brain will store both meanings. Each way we use our information presents an opportunity to build a memory pathway for retrieving it. The more pathways, the greater the likelihood you will be able to recall something when you need it.

Following is a list of easy ways to elaborate your information:

1. Make flash cards and quiz yourself.
2. Draw the information into a concept map. This shows the connections and relationships between the information.
3. Recode the information—that is, put the information into your own words using your own examples. Your brain finds your own words easier to understand and recall.

4. Discuss the information with peers in person or online.
5. Use more than one sense when you study the material. Each sensory pathway creates a memory pathway.
6. Think about how the information connects to you. This elaboration is called the self-reference effect and is particularly powerful (Symons & Johnson, 1997).
7. Make the information into a song. Your brain has been recognizing rhythms and patterns of music your whole life.

Every one of these simple practices is a way to elaborate the information you are trying to learn and recall. Each one of them builds additional memory pathways for the information.

Emotions and Memory

In a fall semester class, I (T. Doyle) showed my students photographs with either neutral emotional content (e.g., cars driving down the road) or highly emotional content (e.g., a starving baby). Through this exercise, I was trying to demonstrate the power of emotional memory on learning. Two years later I mentioned this experiment to my students in an upper-division class, and one of the students raised his hand and said, "That was the starving baby picture." He had seen the picture only once, but two years later he still recalled it with accuracy. This shows that the brain does better remembering emotional content than neutral content (Perrin et al., 2012).

A study by Bloom, Beal, and Kupfer (2003) showed that emotional arousal organizes and coordinates brain activity. When the amygdala (a structure located deep within the brain, primarily responsible for processing memory of emotional reactions) detects emotions, it boosts activity in the areas of the brain that form memories (Gazzaniga, Ivry, & Mangun, 2009). This makes a lot of sense, as all humans have learned that highly emotional events and material are usually important. As learners, anytime you can connect on an emotional level to your new learning by personalizing it or connecting it to an emotional memory, you make it easier to form a memory for the new learning.

Factors That Can Interfere With Memory

In the same way researchers have found ways to improve memory, they have also identified specific actions that can interfere with the formation of memories or the recall of information from memory. Avoiding these memory pitfalls is one key to becoming a more efficient learner.

Multitasking

Most individuals today are good at jumping from one task to another. You can likely be texting someone, listening to music, and doing your math homework—no problem! You might even have the TV on at the same time. Most college students today are better at switching between tasks more rapidly than members of the older generation. However, there is a big difference between switching from one task to another, or task shifting, and *doing* both tasks at the same time, or multitasking. When you shift tasks while working on something that requires thinking, such as texting your friend and listening to a lecture in class, your brain goes through the following steps, which allow you to switch your attention: (a) shift alert: the brain recognizes that you are about to shift your attention; (b) rule activation for task 1: the brain recognizes that you are going to be closing down your current task; (c) disengagement: the brain closes current task; and (d) rule activation for task 2: the brain pays attention to the new task (Medina, 2008). This process is repeated every time you switch tasks that involve thinking, and you never get better or faster at it. Although it is possible to do two things at once, it is not possible to do two cognitively demanding, or thinking, things at the same time. You may have noticed that when you try to do two thinking tasks at the same time, such as listening to two people talk at the same time, you cannot complete both simultaneously, as the brain must shut down one task before working on the other. Typically, individuals who shift tasks make 50% more errors and spend at least 50% more time on both tasks (Medina, 2008). This is a lose-lose situation in that task shifting means it takes longer to do a worse job.

Multitasking violates everything scientists know about good memory formation of new material (Foerde, Knowlton, & Poldrack, 2006). Your brain is at its best when it is focused on one learning task at a time.

Full attention is extremely beneficial for effective learning. One study shows that our brains try to trick us into thinking we can multitask—but we can't (Dux, Ivanoff, Asplund, & Marois, 2006). Focus on one task at a time, and you'll do better at each task in much less time.

Why Students Forget

Everyone forgets things, especially when people are bombarding their brains with stimulation all day long: texting, phoning, e-mailing, posting social media, listening to music, playing video games, watching television, and even studying new information for class. The human brain did not evolve to deal with constant stimulation. Neuroscientist Marc Berman and his colleagues have shown that constant stimulation (walking busy city streets, earphones in all the time with music playing, constant texting, phoning, gaming, etc.) exhausts the brain and causes it to perform more poorly on learning and memory tasks. When our brains are exhausted, it is difficult to remember just about anything (Berman, Jonides, & Kaplan, 2008). Berman and colleagues' research also showed that exhausted brains make for cranky people. The cure is a 20- or 90-minute nap, a quiet walk in the woods (but not the city, which is too full of stimulation), lying in a hammock, or meditation.

Exhaustion contributes to forgetting, but it is not the only factor involved in the failure to remember new information recently learned. In his *The Seven Sins of Memory: How the Mind Forgets and Remembers*, Schacter (2001) notes three main causes of forgetfulness:

1. *Blocking.* Information is stored but can't be accessed at a later time because something is preventing its retrieval. This usually results from anxiety, which causes interference within brain pathways and results in a temporary failure to recall information. Many students have experienced this as test anxiety or when they have been called on to answer questions during class. This may also be experienced when your boyfriend or girlfriend asks if you remember a particular detail regarding your first date.

2. *Misattribution.* A memory is attributed to the wrong situation or source. You might experience this when you tell Pat that you really

enjoyed the dinner you had at a restaurant that is having a grand reopening, only to realize after you spoke that it was Sam you were with on the previous visit. Misattribution may also happen when you are taking two or more courses with similar information during the same semester. Taking biochemistry, biology, and physics at the same time, for example, might cause your brain to confuse which class was the source of which information. To reduce this effect, try studying for each subject in a different room or in a different building or with a different smell present. Then, during the exam, think of where you studied for that examination and get that image in your mind or bring the correct smell with you to the exam.

3. *Transience.* Memory is lost over time, such as phone numbers from years ago or the names of people you knew in grade school or relatives you have not seen in years. With respect to classes, in the first hour following a lecture, 65% of the material presented can be lost. As you have likely experienced, things learned and not used for a long time can be hard to recall. There are ways to reduce this effect. Put in extra study effort when learning the material. Overlearning something greatly diminishes how much of that information is forgotten across time. Another way to reduce the effect is to retrieve the information periodically. Each time you recall information it slows down the forgetting process. It takes much more time and effort to create a lasting memory than most people realize. When you do not practice the information enough over an extended period (distributed practice), your brain has no reason to make long-term memories for the information. When you do not revisit the material for long periods of time, your brain also perceives that the information is no longer needed. There is no substitute for practice, both at the time of learning and then periodically over time.

Caffeine, Sugar, and Memory

In two separate studies, participants who used 75 mg of caffeine and 75 mg of sugar together in drink form were found to show improvement in attention and declarative memory tasks without significant changes in mood (Kennedy & Scholey, 2004). Yes, sugar and caffeine can have beneficial impacts on learning and memory. Of course, it is important to note that sugar and caffeine in excess also lead to negative health outcomes. Increasingly, cases are seen where individuals who have had large doses of caffeine experience seizures (Morrison & Holland, 2016). The point here is that benefits may be realized by using smaller amounts of sugar and caffeine, but there are also some negative outcomes. It is important to note that these benefits may also be obtained through aerobic exercise, which tends to produce enhanced learning along with very good health benefits (see chapter 3).

Stress and Memory

For decades scientists have known that both periodic and long-term stress adversely affect the ability to learn and remember. Only recently was it discovered that even minor stressful events, lasting only a short time, interfere with your ability to learn and remember. Acute stress activates selective corticotrophin-releasing hormones (CRHs), which disrupt the process by which the brain collects and stores memories (Baram, Chen, Dubé, & Burgdorff, 2008). The best way to protect yourself from the hazards of stress is through exercise. A 2012 study showed that aerobic exercise protects the brain from the harmful effects of stress and actually helps the brain repair the damage done from stress (Ebdrup, 2012). Studying regularly over time and knowing the material is also a great defense against stress in the college classroom. Early studying, in fact, has a double effect: You will know the material better through studying early and then practicing retrieving the information periodically, and knowing the material better will reduce stress and make it easier to both learn and then later remember previously learned material.

Memory and Athletics

Most sports require numerous higher-order cognitive abilities and are performed under conditions of extreme stress where the limits of human behavior are being challenged and extended (Furley & Memmert 2010). To use these higher cognitive processes athletes need to master the basic skills of their game, like dribbling in basketball and soccer, throwing in softball or baseball, or passing in football or lacrosse. Mastering the basics makes those actions easier, freeing up athletes' brains to pay additional attention to complex aspects of the game as it is played. That is essentially what is meant when we say a person becomes a professional, or master of a sport. This mastery would include knowing all the plays, sets, and formations, which requires a lot of distributed practice (which we talked at length about in this chapter). The reason coaches run plays over and over is because of what was known even before the research was conducted. The more practice completed, the more automated the play becomes and the less brain energy is required to run it. With current research, we know much more fully why this works. Overlearning frees up the working memory to understand, recognize, and accomplish more complex aspects of the game. If you are busy trying to remember how a play is run, you can't be paying attention to what the defense is doing. This is similar to playing video games. When a new game is learned, the first challenge is to learn the actions that may be completed by the game controller. Once you become very good at the game, you stop thinking about how to use the controller efficiently and spend that cognitive resource on more complex aspects of winning the game.

Once general mastery of skills and plays has been realized, your game performance relies heavily on your working memory. Working memory is what allows us to drive a car while we simultaneously monitor our speed, pay attention to the road ahead, talk to the person in the passenger seat, and check our rearview mirror every few seconds. Similarly, it's also what allows a basketball player to dribble the ball, pay attention to her defender, and keep track of one or two teammates at a time, all while evaluating whether she can or should shoot the ball. It's a huge component of intelligence and high-level performance, no matter the task (Buschman, Siegel, Roy, & Miller, 2011).

Working memory, however, has its limitations. You can pay attention to around four different things in your visual field at once, but only if they are distributed evenly in your visual field (Buschman et al., 2011). Our brains can't handle overload on one side or another; if one side of our visual field gets overloaded, that information just gets lost, and the other side can't pick up the slack (Buschman et al., 2011). The application to sports is significant.

> Let's think about a football quarterback. A quarterback with an average working memory capacity can accurately keep track of and make good decisions about four receivers at a time. This research implies that receiver sets that space receivers more evenly across the quarterback's visual field could optimize his working memory capacity and possibly make it easier for him to find the open man or make good decisions. On the other side of the ball, blitzing defenses might use the strategy of overloading one side of the quarterback's visual field, with the knowledge that it will be nearly impossible for the quarterback to keep track of each defender, due to the limitations of working memory and perception. This knowledge has huge potential to inform play design in football, basketball, or any other sport where manipulating player position could be used to create an advantage based on exploiting the weaknesses of our brain's working memory capacity. (Ponds, deBraek, & Deckers, 2012).

When individuals watch professional sports on television, attend a college game, or participate in intramural competition, most never think of the implications of memory on the performance level of the individual player. As memory is an extremely important component of this performance, however, the person who practices basic plays until they become routine and then learns to focus on more complex aspects of the game has a distinct advantage. In addition, as a person practices fundamental aspects of a sport, those actions are interpreted by the brain as being very important and tend to be remembered very well. This is particularly important in times of high stress. When the game is on the line, you want routine behaviors to be automatic.

Chapter Summary

From learning song lyrics to organic chemistry, there are similar processes to enhancing memory and recall of information. Once you understand these processes you will be able to better understand why you forget and, more importantly, enhance the recall of information you will need at a later time. Following are the key ideas from this chapter:

1. Memories are made during sleep.
2. Naps can help in memory formation and in reducing irritableness.
3. Don't take classes back-to-back. Postexperience rest is important in creating memories for recent experiences.
4. Retrieve a memory to strengthen it. Each time you recall a memory rather than just studying it, your brain makes it stronger and more easily recalled in the future.
5. Cramming may work well in the short run but will not help long-term recall.
6. We remember emotionally charged information better than neutral information.
7. Elaborate information to improve recall. The more ways you practice new information, the more memory pathways are made for recalling it.
8. Don't shift tasks when doing tasks that require thinking or energy. When it comes to learning, your brain is at its best when it is doing one thing at a time.
9. Forgetting is likely a result of anxiety, misattribution, or not practicing the information enough to make it into a more permanent memory.

Critical Thinking and Discussion Questions

1. Why is it detrimental to think to yourself that something is not important or not interesting while you are reading the material? Describe some ways to convince your brain that information learned in a college course is important enough to remember.
2. What do we now know about the importance of sleep memory? If your friend indicates she is exhausted and going to take a 1-hour nap, based on sleep cycles, what would you tell her?

3. What are the short-term and long-term effects of cramming? If cramming does not have good long-term positive outcomes, why do so many students do this so often? If a friend says she does great on unit exams but never does well on the final, what might you tell her based on the information in this chapter?
4. Research on task shifting is very consistent. The next time you study, take note of the number of times you are task shifting. Are you able to focus specifically on the academic task (e.g., reading a chapter, writing a paper, or studying notes), or do you frequently get distracted? What could you do to decrease task shifting?
5. Select and explain three things that increase forgetting. Identify one class you are now taking and explain what you might do, based on information in this chapter, to reduce forgetting of material you are learning.

References

Anwar, Y. (2011, March 8). As we sleep, speedy brain waves boost our ability to learn. *Berkeley News*. Retrieved from http://news.berkeley.edu/2011/03/08/sleep-brainwaves/

Baram, T., Chen, Y., Dubé, C., & Burgdorff, C. (2008, March 13). Short-term stress can affect learning and memory. *Science Daily*. Retrieved from http://www.sciencedaily.com/releases/2008/03/080311182434.htm

Berman, M., Jonides, J., & Kaplan, S. (2008, December). The cognitive benefits of interacting with nature. *Psychological Science, 19*, 1207–1212.

Blasiman, R. N., Dunlosky, J., & Rawson, K. A. (2017). The what, how much, and when of study strategies: Comparing intended versus actual study behavior. *Memory, 25*(6), 784–792.

Bloom, F., Beal, M., & Kupfer, D. (Eds.). (2003). *The Dana guide to brain health*. New York, NY: Free Press.

British Psychological Society (BPS). (2016, December 13). Want to improve your memory? Go to the gym. *Science Daily*. Retrieved from www.sciencedaily.com/releases/2016/12/161213074341.htm

Buschman, T. J., Siegel M., Roy J. E., & Miller, E. K. (2011). Neural substrates of cognitive capacity limitations. *Proceedings of the National Academy of Sciences of the United States of America, 108*(27), 11252–11255.

Buzsáki, G., Girardeau, G., Benchenane, K., Wiener, S., & Zugaro, M. (2009). Selective suppression of hippocampal ripples impairs spatial memory. *Nature Neuroscience, 12*, 1222–1223.

Dunlosky, J., Rawson, K. A., Marsh, E. J., Mitchell, J. N., & Willingham, D. T. (2013). *Improving students' learning with effective learning techniques: Promising directions from cognitive and educational psychology.* Retrieved from www.indiana.edu/~pcl/rgoldsto/courses/dunloskyimprovinglearning.pdf

Dux, P. E., Ivanoff, J., Asplund, C. L. O., & Marois, R. (2006). Isolation of a central bottleneck of information processing with time-resolved fMRI. *Neuron, 52*(6), 1109–1120.

Ebdrup, N. (2012, January 13). Stress and exercise repair the brain after a stroke. *Science Nordic.* Retrieved from http://sciencenordic.com/stress-and-exercise-repair-brain-after-stroke

Feitlinger, S., H. (2017). Pokémon aficionados help scientists prove practice makes perfect. *DOGOnews: ELA-Science-Social Studies.* Retrieved from https://www.dogonews.com/2017/2/6/pokemon-aficionados-help-scientists-prove-practice-makes-perfect/page/4

Foerde, K., Knowlton, B., & Poldrack, R. (2006). Modulation of competing memory systems by distraction. *Proceedings of the National Academy of Sciences of the United States of America, 103*(31), 11778–11783.

Furley, P. A., & Memmert, D. (2010, September). The role of working memory in sport. *International Review of Sport and Exercise Psychology, 3*(2), 171–194.

Gazzaniga, M. S., Ivry, R. B., & Mangun, G. R. (2009). *Cognitive neuroscience: The biology of the mind.* New York, NY: Norton.

Grant, H., Bredahl, H., Clay, J., Ferrie, J., Groves, J., McDormand, T., & Dark, V. (1998). Context-dependent memory for meaningful material: Information for students. *Applied Cognitive Psychology, 12*, 617–623.

Jang, Y., Wixted, T., Pecher, D., Zeelenberg, R., & Huber, D. (2012). Decomposing the interaction between retention interval and study/test practice. *Quarterly Journal of Experimental Psychology, 65*(5), 962–997.

Kansas State University. (2012, June 20). What's your name again? Lack of interest, not brain's ability, may be why we forget. *Science Daily.* Retrieved from www.sciencedaily.com/releases/2012/06/120620113027.htm

Kennedy, D. O., & Scholey, A. B. (2004). A glucose-caffeine energy drink ameliorates subjective and performance deficits during prolonged cognitive demand. *Appetite, 42*, 331–333.

Krishnan, K. (2013). Exam cramming is not learning. *Today.* Retrieved from http://www.todayonline.com/commentary/exam-cramming-not-learning

Levy, R., Levitan, D., & Susswein, A. J. (2016). New learning while consolidating memory during sleep is actively blocked by a protein synthesis dependent process. *eLife*. Retrieved from https://elifesciences.org/articles/17769

Maas, J., & Robbins, R. (2011). *Sleep for success*. Bloomington, IN: Authorhouse.

Mander, B., Santhanam, S., Saletin, R., & Walker, M. (2011). Wake deterioration and sleep restoration of human learning. *Current Biology, 21*(5), R183–R184.

Medina, J. (2008). *Brain rules*. Seattle, WA: Pear Press.

Morrison, W., & Holland, K. (2016). *Common triggers for partial onset seizures.* Retrieved from https://www.healthline.com/health/epilepsy/common-triggers-partial-onset-seizures#Overview1

Naps clear the mind, help you learn. (2010, February 21). *Live Science*. Retrieved from http://www.livescience.com/9819-naps-clear-mind-learn.html

Payne, J. D., Tucker, M. A., Ellenbogen, J. M., Wamsley, E. J., Walker, M. P., Schacter, D. L., & Stickgold, R. (2012). Memory for semantically related and unrelated declarative information: The benefit of sleep, the cost of wake. *PLoS ONE, 7*(3), e33079.

Perrin, M., Henaff, M., Padovan, C., Faillenot, I., Merville, A., & Krolak-Salmon, P. (2012). Influence of emotional content and context on memory in mild Alzheimer's disease. *Journal of Alzheimers Disease, 29*(4), 817–826.

Ponds, R., deBraek, D. & Deckers, K. (2012). *Does working memory training improve the performance of professional football players?* Retrieved from https://www.cogmed.com/working-memory-training-improve-performance-professional-football-players

Rohrer, D., Taylor, K., Pashler, H., Wixted, J. T., & Cepeda, N. J. (2004). The effect of overlearning on long-term retention. *Applied Cognitive Psychology, 19*, 361–374.

Schacter, D. (2001). *Seven sins of memory: How the mind forgets and remembers*. Boston, MA: Houghton Mifflin.

Schlichting, M., & Preston, A. (2014). Memory reactivation during rest supports upcoming learning of related content [Abstract]. *Proceedings of the National Academy of Sciences of the United States of America*. Retrieved from http://www.pnas.org/content/111/44/15845.abstract

Sherkat, M. (2016, December 20). Got to remember them all, Pokémon. *UCR Today*. Retrieved from https://ucrtoday.ucr.edu/43127

Shibata, K., Sasaki, Y., Bang, J., Walsh, E., Machizawa, M., Tamaki, M., . . . Watanabe, T. (2017). Overlearning hyperstabilizes a skill by rapidly making neurochemical processing inhibitory-dominant. *Nature Neuroscience, 20*(3), 470–475.

Squire, L. R., & Kandel, E. R. (2000). *Memory: From Mind to Molecules.* New York, NY: Scientific American Library.

Symons, C. T., & Johnson, B. T. (1997). The self-reference effect in memory: A meta-analysis. *Psychological Bulletin, 121*, 371–394.

Tambini, A., Ketz, N., & Davachi, L. (2010). Enhanced brain correlations during rest are related to memory for recent experiences. *Neuron, 65*(2), 280–290.

Tauber, S., Witherby, A., Dunlosky, J., Rawsom, K., Putnam, A., & Roediger, H. (2017). Does covert retrieval benefit learning of key-term definitions? *Journal of Applied Research on Memory and Cognition.* Retrieved from http://www.sciencedirect.com/science/article/pii/S2211368116301292

University of California, Berkeley. (2011, March 8). Brain's learning ability seems to recharge during light slumber [News release]. *Health Day.* Retrieved from https://consumer.healthday.com/cognitive-health-information-26/brain-health-news-80/brain-s-learning-ability-seems-to-recharge-during-light-slumber-650627.html

Walker, M. (2005). A refined model of sleep and the time course of memory formation. *Behavioral and Brain Science, 28*, 51–104.

Wheeler, M. A., Ewers, M., & Buonanno, J. F. (2003). Different rates of forgetting following study versus test trials. *Memory, 11*, 571–580.

Xie, W., & Zhang, W. (2016). Familiarity increases the number of remembered Pokémon in visual short-term memory. *Memory & Cognition, 45*(4), 677–689.

7

MINDSET TOWARD LEARNING

When a college or university sends you an acceptance letter, they are also letting you know they believe you are smart enough to graduate from that institution. Even if you attend an open admission college or a community college, they still hold this general belief that you can be successful. Every institution in higher education has support services for those who struggle—again, because they feel that individuals will need assistance from time to time, but that everyone in their college or university has the ability to succeed. If they didn't believe this, they would not have accepted you as it would be unethical to take your money if they felt you had no chance to succeed.

Unfortunately, nearly 40% of first-year students admitted end up not graduating with a 4-year degree, even when given 6 years to finish (National Center for Educational Statistics, 2015). It's not due to intelligence. With the exceptions of illness or financial difficulty, we believe that the determiner of whether you will or will not walk across the stage and receive your diploma depends almost totally on just five basic things:

1. Your willingness to spend the significant amount of time and effort that it takes to learn and remember the skills, behaviors, and content of your courses
2. Your willingness to take learning risks that challenge you to grow as a learner
3. Your willingness to learn from failures, even for things beyond your control, and make adjustments as you progress
4. Your belief in yourself that you can learn, even though it will be challenging at times
5. Your ability to celebrate successes in your academic progress and build on your belief in your own future abilities

Time, effort, risk, learning from failure (a valuable experience when learning, and an opportunity for growth), and believing in yourself will get you to the graduation ceremony in your very own cap and gown. Believing you can make it, and then putting in the work is critical. This chapter is about the beliefs people hold about their own intelligence and how these beliefs determine the extent to which a person will do the five things required to reach graduation.

Mindset and Learning

The goal of this chapter is to help you come to better understand yourself as a learner. Through this understanding we believe you will experience a fundamental change in the way you learn. Gaining this understanding is so important that it will likely influence many other aspects of your life as well. The information in this chapter relates to a concept researchers call mindset. A mindset is a view you have of yourself as a learner, and it affects all the decisions you make about your learning. Mindset was first described by Carol Dweck, a psychologist at Stanford University. Dweck explains that your view of yourself as a learner was likely formed in middle school (or even earlier) and although you may not know it, your mindset has been affecting your learning ever since (Dweck, 2006, 2009). As you read this chapter, reflect on the concepts presented and try to figure out what kind of mindset you have and how you can develop a mindset that leads to optimal learning for you.

Mindset and Intelligence

One thing about human intelligence is certain: It is malleable, meaning intelligence is changed through exposure to new information or even by looking at what you already know in a new way. There is no limit to what you can learn, and contrary to what some may think, nobody's brain has ever been shown to be "filled." The brain continually changes by making new neuroconnections between its cells, which represent new knowledge or skills, and when this happens, we say someone has learned something. It is possible for humans to learn all the time and in any area of study. You have already learned millions of bits of information. Think about all you know about your family, your friends, different products, and how to get to around town. These constitute only a small sample of all you have learned. You should never think you can't learn, because you are doing it literally all of the time. That said, with respect to college and university classes, although learning anything is possible, some subjects will certainly be more difficult for you to learn than others. Intelligence is not a fixed quantity that you got at birth and are stuck with for your entire life. Smartness is not something you have or don't have. It is something you work at all of the time. You become smarter every day. The amount of information you amass in your lifetime is inconceivable. That said, if you have the wrong mindset about learning something in particular, it will have a heavy impact on how much you will learn—and just about everything else in your life.

Your mindset is your view of your own intelligence and abilities. This view affects your willingness to engage in learning tasks and how much, if any, effort you are willing to expend to meet a learning challenge. Dweck has spent more than 30 years researching learners' mindsets and their individual views of their intelligence. She noted that an individual's mindset falls into one of two categories: fixed mindsets and growth mindsets. A person with a fixed mindset about something "believes that intelligence is a fixed trait" (Dweck, 2006, p. 7) despite hundreds of studies that have found otherwise. In this view, either you are smart in a given area or you are not; there is nothing you can do to improve in that area. Individuals with fixed mindsets believe their intelligence is reflected in their academic performance. If a student doesn't do well in a class, it's because he or she is not "smart" in that area. Individuals with fixed mindsets have a mistaken belief that they shouldn't need to work hard to do well because the smart students don't have to—although when researchers asked students who consistently achieved high grades they reported working very hard on academic material—or that putting in the effort won't make any difference in the outcome ("I'm just not good at math," "I can't give presentations," "I am a terrible writer," or "I am no good at sports"). In fact, individuals with fixed mindsets often see putting in effort as an indication that they are not smart. After all, as their mistaken belief holds, you either have it or you don't, so to work at something shows you don't have it naturally. They have falsely concluded that learning comes easily to the students at the top of the class.

People with growth mindsets, in contrast, believe that intelligence grows as you add new knowledge and skills. Those with growth mindsets value hard work, learning, and challenges and see failure as a message that they need to change tacks in order to succeed next time. Thomas Edison is reported to have tried hundreds of times before he got the lightbulb to work. At one point, he was asked by a *New York Times* reporter about all his failures and whether he was going to give up. Edison responded, "I have not failed 700 times. I've succeeded in proving 700 ways how not to build a light bulb" (as cited in Ferlazzo, 2011, para. 3). Shortly after this interview, he was successful, and we have all since benefited from his growth mindset. Individuals with growth mindsets are willing to take learning risks and understand that through practice and effort—sometimes a lot of effort—their abilities can improve. Those with growth mindsets believe that their brains are malleable, that intelligence and abilities constantly grow, and that only time will tell how smart they will become. The next time you start to think, "I can't ____," move to a growth mindset and say to yourself, "I can't _____ yet."

Chess Champions

In 2008 three British researchers set out to discover what people who became extraordinary in their fields had in common. One of the groups they looked at were the top-10 chess players in the world. One of the criteria they used in their investigation was general intelligence, or IQ. The researchers had each of the 10 expert chess players take an intelligence test. They were surprised to discover three of the chess players had below-average IQs. They pondered the obvious question: How could a person be so good at a complex game, which most associate with high intelligence, yet have a low IQ? The answer they found explained how a person becomes an expert: practice. Each of the three players with below-average IQs had played between 10,000 and 50,000 hours of chess. Their effort and practice had allowed them to become much better chess players than thousands of other chess players who had higher levels of intelligence. We now know that every time you practice something it becomes just a bit easier to do it again in the future. The first time you walked across campus it was a bit confusing. Each time it becomes easier and easier. The same is true for tying your shoes, playing a video game, shooting a basket, and solving algebra problems. It may take many trials, as it did with chess players, but even if practice does not make perfect, it does at least make it better. The discovery of the benefits of practice among chess players led researchers to identify many additional cases in which greatness was achieved through thousands of hours and years of practice (Colvin, 2006).

Those studying learning and memory now agree that it is not typically intelligence that makes a person an expert in a given area, but rather effort and practice. Think of a case in which an individual stepped into the spotlight and won a competition, whether it was basketball, race-car driving, chess, or a quiz bowl. It doesn't just happen. In fact, in most news interviews, top athletes commonly talk about how hard they have been working on their game. George Gervin, one of the highest scorers in National Basketball Association (NBA) history, was known for shooting a thousand jump shots every day. Whether you want to be skilled at an activity or a top scholar in your discipline, having a growth mindset and taking the time to practice are necessary.

The Beginning: Middle School

An individual's mindset begins to surface in middle school, when more rigorous academic work appears in the curriculum. Students who in elementary school could be successful with little effort and students who were frequently told they were "naturally smart" begin to doubt their abilities when learning challenges increase and failure happens on some tasks. Dweck discovered that these students had abilities that inspired learner self-confidence, but only when the going was easy. When setbacks occurred, everything changed. Dweck, with her colleague Elaine Elliott, discovered that learning goals explained the difference between students who were not stopped by the setbacks and those who saw setbacks as failures to be avoided or as insurmountable barriers. "The mastery-oriented students [those with growth mindsets] are really hell-bent on learning something" and have strong "learning goals" (Dweck, 2007a). Learning goals are different from performance goals in an important way. Performance goals are oriented on a specific task, whereas learning goals consider the bigger picture of what is being learned through both success and failure. Failures often deter students for whom performance is paramount in an attempt to look smart even if it means not learning in the process. These individuals have a fixed mindset and will even put others down when failures happen in order to preserve their self-esteem. For them, each task is a challenge to their self-image, and each setback becomes a personal threat. Often, they pursue only activities at which they're sure to shine—and they avoid the sorts of experiences necessary to grow and flourish in any endeavor (Dweck, 2006).

Dweck (2006) is careful to point out that learning mindsets are context-specific. That is, a person can have a growth mindset in one area and a fixed mindset in another area. You might believe that you cannot do math because you weren't born with "math smarts" and that working harder or getting extra help won't help you to learn math. You might also take guitar lessons and practice on your guitar 3 hours a day because you know practice is needed to be good at playing a guitar. In this case, you would hold a fixed mindset for math and a growth mindset for guitar playing. There is no doubt that people have preferences; you may well like playing the guitar and not like math. Sometimes, the preferences come from being good at something, which comes from practice. This makes learning a very circular process. With respect to intelligence and abilities, practicing math for 3 hours every night for a few months would greatly change your math intelligence and likely change how you feel about math in the process. Another surprising finding from Dweck's (2006) research is that there is no relationship between students' abilities or intelligence and the development of a growth mindset. Sometimes students with all As have fixed mindsets. One bright student might develop a fixed mindset while another develops a growth mindset based on the feedback each has received about their past performances and current levels of ability. A student with a fixed mindset may have had early successes at math and may have received feedback such as "You are really smart!" or "You are a natural at math. You should be a mathematics teacher!" These types of comments might have given that student the impression that certain subjects come easily to smart people. If you have to work at learning, they surmise, then you are not smart. This feedback might give a person a fixed mindset for math. The problem often comes later, when the math becomes more difficult and hard work is needed to be successful. Now the student might think, "I must not be good at this type of math. Oh, well, when it comes to math you either have it or you don't, and I was good at algebra, I am just not good at advanced math. I guess I will do something else." This is also the foundation of why some students who struggle in their first semester at college say, "I was high school smart; I am just not college smart." Nothing shuts down progress faster than a fixed mindset person who struggles.

Students who have a fixed mindset and quit at the first signs of failure might have had very different outcomes if his or her early success was met with growth-mindset-encouraging comments such as "Look at how well you did. Your hard work really paid off." This feedback fosters a growth mindset and encourages practice in the future, which often leads to more success and a stronger growth mindset. If you are a nontraditional student who has children, you might follow Dweck's advice for parents. She says it is vital for parents to give feedback on their children's successful efforts and learning strategies, not on their intelligence (Dweck, 2006). The significance of Dweck's research for college students is profound. Each fall, tens of thousands of students enroll in courses that they believe they cannot pass. They also believe that hiring a tutor, visiting the professor during office hours for extra help, or even working harder will make no difference. They hold this false belief because they have a fixed mindset in that area, and as a result often do not do well in these courses. If their mindset does not change, the extra help is not likely to lead to success.

The next time you take a class on a subject you fear because you think you are not "smart" in that area, keep in mind that practice can make a huge difference in your learning success. The class will likely not be easy for you, but if you take time to gain the background knowledge (e.g., through use of the writing center, learning development courses, or tutoring) and you work hard (keep a growth mindset), there is no telling what you will achieve.

Fixed Mindsets and Perceived Laziness

College and university professors often see lack of effort as laziness. Not going to tutoring or taking advantage of a professor's office hours is seen as irresponsible or immature. In fact, it may be that a student's fixed mindset is causing many of his or her problems. If you have always struggled with reading, you may believe it is because you are simply "bad at reading" or "not smart in that way." The same may be true of math, giving presentations, taking tests, or writing term papers. A person with a fixed mindset in some area sees tutoring and extra work as wasted effort. Other students with similar mindsets may work hard but tell themselves, "This is hard. . . . I can't get it. . . . Maybe I should drop the class." We don't have to tell you that studying with that attitude is not productive. There is simply no way to concentrate on the task of learning something difficult if you are also thinking that you cannot learn the material. In contrast, those with growth mindsets work hard, even on work for classes they don't like. Because they know the effort will likely produce improved results, they can focus their energy on learning, and as a result, they see greater success. Those students are not smarter; they just see themselves differently.

Characteristics of Fixed and Growth Mindsets

Following is a list of behaviors for each type of mindset. These lists have been included to help you discover how you view yourself as a learner in the many different areas of your learning life. These lists were compiled based on information from Michael Richard (2007).

Fixed Mindset

1. *Self-image.* Just about everyone strives to have a positive self-image, even those with fixed mindsets. How do individuals with fixed mindsets, who fail to see value in working to improve, protect their self-image? They take only easy tasks, try to make others look dumb, and discount others' achievements.

2. *Challenges.* Students with fixed mindsets often stick to what they know they can do well. They avoid other challenges because the potential for failure presents a risk to their self-image. If you are a student who asks, "What are the easiest classes I can take?" you may have a fixed mindset.

3. *Obstacles.* People with fixed mindsets usually use obstacles—or external, uncontrollable roadblocks that make learning harder and are difficult to avoid—as an excuse for failure or avoid these situations by just being absent.

4. *Effort.* People with fixed mindsets view effort as unpleasant and unrewarding; therefore, it is to be avoided. Their perception of "great effort" can fall quite short of what is required to achieve academic success. This may also contribute to their view of effort as futile.

5. *Criticism.* For people with fixed mindsets, any criticism of their abilities is seen as criticism of themselves as individuals. Useful criticism is usually ignored or, even worse, seen as an insult. This personal response to criticism leads to less and less chance of improvement because they are not open to using any of the feedback that could help them improve.

6. *Success of others.* Students with fixed mindsets see others' success as making them look bad. They may try to convince their peers that others' success was attributable to luck, an expensive private tutor, or even cheating. They may even try to distract their peers from the success of others by bringing up their own unrelated personal successes or the previous failures of those who are currently successful.

Growth Mindset

1. *Self-image.* Individuals with growth mindsets do not see their self-image as tied to their abilities because they know their abilities can be further developed and improved. They want to learn and accept that failure is an important part of learning, even if they are not creating the lightbulb.

2. *Challenges.* Those with growth mindsets embrace challenges because they believe they will come out stronger for being tested. They believe they will discover valuable things by engaging in the effort of a challenge.

3. *Obstacles.* Because the self-image of a person with a growth mindset is not tied to his or her success or the opinion of others, failure is an opportunity to learn. So, in a sense, these people win either way. An obstacle is just one more of many things on the road toward learning and improving.

4. *Effort.* People with growth mindsets see effort as necessary if growth and eventual mastery is to be achieved. It is viewed as a natural part of the learning process.

5. *Criticism.* Students with growth mindsets do not like to receive negative criticism any more than anyone else, but they know it is

not personal and that it is meant to help them grow and improve. They also see the criticism as directed only at their current level of abilities, which they know will change with time and effort.

6. *Success of others.* The success of others is seen as an inspiration, and their information findings are seen as something to learn from.

Changing to a Growth Mindset

Nearly everyone has at least one fixed mindset, and there are things you can do to change your fixed mindsets into growth mindsets. As was mentioned at the beginning of this chapter, intelligence is malleable and can be changed, meaning you can, in fact, grow your brain. Jesper Mogensen (2012), a psychologist at the University of Copenhagen, has found that the brain is like a muscle that gets stronger with use and that learning prompts neurons in the brain to grow new connections. You need to understand that you are an agent of your own brain development.

Dweck's (2007a) research has found that students of all ages, from early grade school through college, can learn to have growth mindsets. It is important to recognize that your intellectual skills can be cultivated through hard work, reading, education, the confrontation of challenges, and other activities. Dweck explains that students may know how to study, but they won't want to if they believe their efforts are futile. If you accept that effort will pay dividends, then you are on your way to greater academic and life success. This does not mean that you will enjoy all subjects that you study—only that everyone can improve as they work in different academic areas. Every teacher was a novice at one time and had to spend a good deal of time studying in order to become an expert in his or her field. Those who are good at sports had to practice extensively, and individuals who are accomplished artists work at details of their art over and over. Researcher Joshua Aronson of New York University demonstrated that college students' GPAs go up when they accept that intelligence can be developed (cited in Dweck, 2007b). Following are several aspects of a growth mindset that are important for you to know:

1. Success most often comes from effort and learning strategies, not intelligence. If intelligence earned you a grade of A on the first test and then you failed the second test, did you suddenly become stupid? Of course not. For the first test, you used the right study strategies and put in enough effort to earn an A. When you failed, something was wrong with your level of effort and strategy. It may be that the material was more difficult and needed additional effort.

2. You can grow your own brain. Neuroscience research findings clearly show that new neuron networks are created and become permanent through effort and practice (Goldberg, 2009; Ratey, 2001). These new networks make us smarter. This knowledge is the key to shifting yourself away from a fixed mindset toward a growth mindset.

3. Failure can point you toward future success. When you fail, focus on the strategies you used and the time and effort you put forth to see what caused the failure. Ask for feedback from the teacher. Taking advantage of failure is a key ingredient in creating a growth mindset. When you focus on how you can improve—by finding a new strategy, getting a study partner, reviewing on a daily basis, or putting in more time and effort—you can discover how to overcome the failure. Your ability to face a challenge is not dependent on your actual skills or abilities; it's based on the mindset you bring to the challenge. You need to be willing to take learning risks and remain open to learning all you can from your experiences. This message can be difficult to accept, but it is crucial to your growth and development as a learner.

4. Your performance reflects only your current skills and efforts, not your intelligence, worth, or potential. Weight-lifting improvement comes solely from improved technique and increased effort. The more you practice and the better your technique becomes, the greater the amount of weight you can lift. Being a weakling is simply a current state of performance, not who you are. College classes are often like weight lifting. You start small, and with repeated practice, you keep building brain muscle.

How Can You Help Yourself?

The answer is to use productive and positive growth-minded self-talk. Carol Dweck (2009) offers several suggestions.

Step 1. Learn to Hear Your Fixed Mindset "Voice"

Students can learn to listen and recognize when they are engaging in a fixed mindset. Students may say to themselves or hear in their heads things like "Are you sure you can do it? Maybe you don't have the talent" or "What if you fail—you'll be a failure." Also, catch yourself exaggerating the situation, as that can signal a fixed mindset. Some individuals indicate they can't do math. Geometry, algebra, and calculus are challenging for everyone at the beginning. Like basketball or drawing, it takes a great deal of practice. Also, some individuals make the mistake of calling anything with numbers math and will indicate the fixed mindset statement that "they can't do math," meaning any math. For those individuals, as soon as a task includes numbers, they shut down. In truth, everyone can do some math. As an example, if your roommate says, "I can't to math," ask him a very simple question, such as "What is 1 + 2?" What you are likely to find is that he can do simple addition but struggles with statistics. There is a difference between addition, trigonometry, geometry, calculus, and statistics. Start with less complex concepts and practice; that is the way people learn math. The same is true in many areas. As noted previously, it isn't helpful to use the fixed mindset phrase, "I can't give presentations." Instead, try "I can't give presentations as well as I would like at this time."

Step 2. Recognize You Have a Choice

How you interpret challenges, setbacks, and criticism is a choice. You need to know you can choose to ramp up your strategies and effort, stretch yourself, and expand your abilities. It's up to you.

Step 3. Talk Back to Yourself With a Growth Mindset Voice

THE FIXED MINDSET says, "Are you sure you can do it? Maybe you don't have the talent."

THE GROWTH MINDSET answers, "I'm not sure I can do it now, but I think I can learn to with time and effort."
FIXED MINDSET: "If you fail—you'll be a failure."
GROWTH MINDSET: "Failure is information on how to get better."

Step 4. Take Growth Mindset Action

The more you choose the growth mindset voice, the easier it will become to choose it again and again. Success comes slowly, and it can be frustrating. That said, the only way to get good at anything is to practice, and failure is going to happen when you push yourself to new levels.

Mindset and Athletics

For athletes to reach their athletic potential, they must have a growth mindset. They must come to realize that nothing relating to ability is fixed, and potential performance is determined not by who you are, but by what you do (O'Sullivan, 2014).

If you follow baseball you realize that even the best baseball hitters fail to hit seven out of every 10 times they come to bat. Most soccer games have so few goals scored that the persons who score even one goal a game become stars, even though they may have tried and failed to score eight to 10 times during a game. Every volley in tennis results in someone missing a shot. Failure is common in all sports, and learning from failure is a key to success. That learning comes from a growth mindset.

Successful athletes spend a lot of time reviewing their errors and failures to figure out what they did wrong and how to do better. Professional players watch past performances of both themselves and their competition to study ways to be better. These are athletes that have a growth mindset. Successful athletes take their coaches' criticism as feedback on how to improve and recognize that the criticism reflects only their current state of play and not how good they might become. Good players constantly ask for this feedback from their coaches and see a lack of feedback as a bad thing. These are athletes who have a growth mindset.

The classroom and the playing field are similar in that in order to get good at anything you need to practice and recognize that you won't get everything correct. You can't stop just because you are successful once. It is important to overlearn. You should not expect to practice until you get it right, but practice until you can't get it wrong. Your mindset is one of the most powerful tools for improving your athletic ability. To get better, you need to see yourself as always having the ability to get better through hard work, new strategies, better training, or new instruction. Most importantly, those who learn something every time they fail at sports, and then do something to get better next time, are the players who end up the best in their respective fields.

Chapter Summary

1. A mindset is a view you have of yourself as a learner, and it affects all the decisions you make about your learning—the effort you put forth, the risks you take, how you deal with failures and criticism, and how much of a challenge you are willing to accept.

2. Mindset was first described by Carol Dweck (2006), a psychologist at Stanford University. Dweck explains that this view of yourself as a learner was likely formed in middle school (or even earlier) and has been affecting your learning ever since.

3. One thing about human intelligence is certain: It is malleable, meaning it can be changed through exposure to new information or even by looking at what you already know in a new way. There is no limit to what you can learn, contrary to what some may think.

4. Dweck (2006) noted that individuals' views of themselves as learners fall into two categories: fixed mindsets and growth mindsets.

5. Those with fixed mindsets believe that intelligence is a fixed trait. In their view, you are either smart in a given area or you are not, and nothing can be done to improve in that area. Students with fixed mindsets usually put forth much less effort in their course if the course is viewed as difficult because they believe they are not smart enough to pass.

6. People with growth mindsets believe that intelligence grows as you add new knowledge and skills. They value hard work, learning, and challenges and see failure as a message that they need to change tacks in order to succeed next time.

7. These views of intelligence begin to surface in middle school, when more rigorous academic work appears in the curriculum.

8. Dweck (2006) is careful to point out that these mindsets are context-specific. That is, a person can have a growth mindset in one area and a fixed mindset in another area.

9. A fixed mindset, which often causes students to put in less effort and to avoid going to tutoring or using a professor's office hours, is often mischaracterized by college and university professors as laziness, irresponsibility, or immaturity. Students with fixed mindsets often take on only easy tasks, try to make others look dumb, and discount others' achievements to protect their self-image.

10. Jesper Mogensen (2012), a psychologist at the University of Copenhagen, has found that the brain is like a muscle that gets stronger with use and that learning prompts neurons in the brain to grow new connections. You need to understand that you are an agent of your own brain development.

11. When you fail, focus on the strategies you used and the time and effort you put forth to see what caused the failure. Ask for feedback from the teacher. This is a key ingredient in creating a growth mindset.

Critical Thinking and Discussion Questions

1. Select three characteristics of a fixed mindset and three characteristics of a growth mindset. Describe a time in your life when you experienced each of these. What was the task and how did you feel about what you were doing?

2. Describe something that you feel you do very well. Next, note one thing about whatever it is that you described that the average person would not know. How did you become proficient or good at what

you described? How did you learn that one thing you just described that the average person wouldn't know? What are you working on currently to become even better at that which you described?

3. Describe at least one thing for which you have a fixed mindset. Why do you think you have a fixed mindset for this thing and yet not for other things? Where did that mindset come from?

4. Criticism, and even feedback in general, is difficult for some people. How do you tend to respond to critiques of your work? In general, do you feel as though the feedback reflects you or your performance? How can you change your mindset concerning feedback in the future?

5. Suppose you asked a friend to play on your intramural soccer team, which is not an excessively competitive team. You know he is a good runner, but he says, "I am terrible at sports." What might you say to your friend to help him get better at, and enjoy, playing on your intramural soccer team?

References

Colvin, G. (2006, October 19). What it takes to be great. *Fortune*. Retrieved from http://money.cnn.com/magazines/fortune/fortune_archive/2006/10/30/8391794/index.htm

Dweck, C. S. (2006). *Mindset: The new psychology of success*. New York, NY: Random House.

Dweck, C. S. (2007a). Interview by Lisa Trei [Video]. *Stanford News*. Retrieved from http://news.stanford.edu/news/2007/february7/videos/179.html

Dweck, C. S. (2007b, July 29). The secret to raising smart kids. *Scientific American*. Retrieved from https://www.scientificamerican.com/article/the-secret-to-raising-smart-kids1/

Dweck, C. S. (2009). Mindset: Powerful insights. *Positive Coaching Alliance*. Retrieved from http://www.positivecoach.org/carol-dweck.aspx

Ferlazzo, L. (2011, June 11). What is the accurate Edison quote on learning from failure? [Web log post]. Retrieved from http://larryferlazzo.edublogs.org/2011/06/11/what-is-the-accurate-edison-quote-on-learning-from-failure/

Goldberg, E. (2009). *The new executive brain: Frontal lobes in a complex world.* New York, NY: Oxford University Press.

Mogensen, J. (2012). Cognitive recovery and rehabilitation after brain injury: Mechanisms, challenges and support. In A. Agrawal (Ed.), *Brain injury— Functional aspects, rehabilitation and prevention* (pp. 121–150). Rijeka, Croatia: InTech.

National Center for Educational Statistics. (2015). *Graduation rates.* Retrieved from https://nces.ed.gov/fastfacts/display.asp?id=40

O'Sullivan, J. (2014). The mindset of high performers. *Changing the Game project.* Retrieved from http://changingthegameproject.com/the-mindset-of-high-performers/

Ratey, J. (2001). *A user's guide to the brain.* New York, NY: Pantheon.

Richard, M. (2007, May). Fixed mindset vs. growth mindset: Which one are you? [Web log post]. Retrieved from http://michaelgr.com/2007/04/15/fixed-mindset-vs-growth-mindset-which-one-are-you/

8

PAYING ATTENTION

In many respects, attention can be thought of as the foundation of all learning. Attention is your awareness that something is happening in the world around you. It is the result of neurons firing because of something that hits your senses. It may be something you see, hear, feel, or smell. Simply put, if your neurons are not stimulated enough to catch your attention, then in your world, it never happened. Perhaps because of the importance of gathering information to facilitate your survival, your brain is an attention-seeking device. Your brain is always looking for information in your environment. Thousands of years ago a rustling bush might have indicated the threat of a tiger that was looking for meat; today a gap in a line of moving cars represents a safe time to cross the street. You attend to books to learn course material and the tone of your friend's voice to gauge whether what he said was serious or a joke. With all this constant attending to stimuli it is easy to get exhausted, so you must also know when to take a break from information gathering. The process of quieting your brain, such as with meditation, takes tremendous energy and practice.

When it comes to learning in your academic courses, you have likely noticed how hard it is to learn anything when you are bored.

Even simple material becomes difficult to learn when you are not interested. In these cases, your mind wanders, looking for something more interesting and challenging. Challenging material may also make your brain wander, perhaps as you think about how difficult the material is rather than attending to the material itself. Overall, attention can be a very challenging thing to control. When you are interested in something you will naturally pay attention. When bored or frustrated, your brain wanders and you likely start to think about other things and that is when you are most likely to reach for your phone out of habit. With respect to learning: If something doesn't catch your attention, you can't learn anything new about it.

Attention and Learning

How many times have you heard a teacher or your parents say, "I need your full attention" or "Pay attention to me when I am talking to you"? They do that because, even though you might not realize it, they can tell that your brain has gone looking for more interesting alternative material and you are not attending to what they deem as important at that time. This might be frustrating to you, but when it comes to learning anything new, you must attend to the incoming information. Unfortunately, paying attention to something is not as easy as it would seem. The human brain is wired to attend to whatever is most interesting at a given time and to hold that attention until something causes the attention to shift to something else. The amount of time before you shift attention is largely determined by past experiences and your past experiences are unique to you. As you live your life, your brain is wired by all the experiences that you encounter. Because every human has had a unique set of experiences, our brains are all wired differently. Even identical twins do not have identical brains because their experiences are different. This wiring process directly influences your attention span. If you are under the age of 30 you have lived your entire life in a media-based culture that is full of short bursts of information (television commercials, music videos, text messages, e-mails, tweets, etc.) that have wired your brain to deal with information that grabs your attention for short periods and, for most people, almost continu-ally. People who lived before the intense media coverage seen today had brains wired to deal with information delivered less frequently and spread out over longer periods of time. For example, researchers have found that the average political sound bite is now only about 8 seconds. This has changed considerably over the past 50 years. During the 1968 presidential election, the average sound bite was a full 43 seconds. By the 1990s, CBS began to resist this tendency to very short sound bites by stating that they would not broadcast any sound bite less than 30 seconds. Eliminating short sound bites was proposed as an effort to better promote informed, complex discourse. Two decades later, the trend continues toward very short sound bites. At this time candidates for public office are cut off very quickly to keep average viewers' attention. It is not possible to explain complex ideas in an 8-second sound bite (Montagne, 2011).

Information is coming at all of us at an amazing pace, particu-larly as compared to our ancestors. A person living in the 1850s would experience in his or her entire lifetime about the same amount of information that you could gain from reading the *New York Times* for one week. Because information is spread so rapidly and so frequently today, our brains must respond in very different ways from how they would have even a few decades ago. According to a July 2010 article published in the medical journal *Pediatrics*, increased exposure to tel-evision and video games has caused a noticeable decrease in attention spans in schoolchildren (Swing, Gentile, Anderson, & Walsh, 2010). A 2015 Canadian study of 2,000 young people found that since the year 2000 the average sustained attention span of young people has dropped from 12 seconds to 8 seconds, which is actually less than the attention span of a goldfish (McSpadden, 2015). This means that because of this constant barrage of information, it takes effort to stay on task without letting something divert your attention. The increase of instant media availability like cell phones will make it more and more difficult to sustain attention. In the same Canadian study just noted 77% of participants aged 18 to 24 agreed with the following statement: "When nothing is occupying my attention, the first thing I do is reach for my phone."

There is also evidence to show that multitasking (actually task shifting) does damage to important alertness capabilities, as it encourages you to shift your attention frequently (Carp, Fitzgerald, Taylor, & Weissman,, 2012). There are many ways in which we learn, and these days one thing we are learning is to have shorter and shorter attention spans. In other words, in the lightning-fast, multimedia society we've become, where individuals study while watching TV, texting friends, and tweeting, the attention span may be an endangered species. And like any endangered species, special work must be done to nurture and improve your attention span in order to ensure its survival and with it your learning success.

Types of Attention

We all know paying attention and holding that attention to learn are crucial to college success. But what exactly does it mean to "pay attention"? It turns out there is disagreement among researchers about what is meant by the concept of attention. We all tend to use the term *attention* to mean one thing, but researchers differentiate between different types of attention: focused, sustained, effortless, and effortful. *Focused attention* is very short in duration, perhaps only a few seconds. This type of attention usually refers to attending to an immediate need like answering the phone, opening a door, or figuring out what just startled you. This kind of attention has changed little in humans over time. *Sustained attention* kicks in when you need to pay attention to something for a longer period of time (Dawson & Medler, 2009). This kind of attention is needed to do tasks that require attention for many minutes to several hours. To read a book, watch a movie, complete a group assignment in class, or learn from a course lecture you will need sustained attention. Sustained attention is extremely important in college. Unfortunately, this type of attention has shortened in span considerably in recent years, making it difficult for you and your friends to stay focused in class or while doing homework.

The research literature also refers to *effortless attention*, often referred to as "being in the flow" or "in the zone." This usually occurs while engaged in an activity you find challenging but enjoyable and where your skills match the demands of the activity. In this situation, your mind enters a groove of exceptionally focused, and yet effortlessly maintained, attention (Bruya, 2010; Csikszentmihalyi, 2014). You may have experienced this kind of attention when winning at a sport where you have a lot of skill, while playing a video game that you are very good at, or during a long run. Some individuals are lucky enough to experience this type of focused attention while learning. This could come from reading a book, writing programming code, or working on an exciting research project. If you find yourself losing track of time and having fun while completing a task or learning experience, you might well be experiencing "flow."

Finally, there is *effortful attention*, which is often needed when you read a difficult book or participate in class on a topic that may not be a primary area of interest for you. This type of attention is described in the dual-process model of attention and action control theory. What is meant by the "dual processes" of attention and action control is that to be successful you have to increase your effort in direct relation to the demands for the control of attention (Osman, 2004). Essentially, as the skills or learning tasks get more difficult, you need to pay more attention to understand and learn the material. This is clearly a very important kind of attention for college and high school students as classroom learning can be difficult (or boring to you) for a variety of reasons. Understanding that to learn you have to pay attention and that some learning situations will require you to increase your attention as the task gets harder are two crucial keys to your learning success.

Learning, Attention, and Boredom

In 1977, I (T. Doyle) read Richard Bach's book published that same year, *Illusions: The Adventures of a Reluctant Messiah,* in which he suggested that true learning requires the learner to sacrifice boredom, giving it up as an excuse for not doing well academically (or in other aspects of life). Bach also said that it was not an easy sacrifice to make. This message has stuck with me ever since. Boredom is a choice, but choosing to seek out and engage in an activity when you are bored by it takes energy. People, books, movies, and lectures by professors are not inherently boring. Many factors contribute to what you think is boring and what you find interesting, and what you find fascinating may well be boring to someone else. For the most part, humans find things boring if they are too simplistic or too difficult to comprehend. It is the challenging yet reachable things that are typically seen as interesting. Sometimes, when you have to learn something you think is boring, the trick is to figure out some challenging or interesting aspect of the material.

Have you ever been in what you would describe as an exceptionally boring class? Of course—we all have. The crucial question is "Did everyone fail that class?" Courses in which everyone fails are extremely rare. So how do students pass a course, perhaps even earn an A, when the material is so boring that paying attention to it is extremely challenging? Typically, successful students put aside their disinterest and force themselves to pay attention because they know they need to learn in spite of the teacher's behavior. It is crucial that you understand that *you do not have the luxury in college to pay attention only to what interests you.* This last statement is so important that it may be the difference between earning academic success and failing out of college. Sometimes, you have to bring meaning and challenge to the material to increase your interest and attention. When it comes to learning, you need greater goals, such as graduation or the feeling of personal accomplishment, to motivate you to pay attention. Remember: The one absolute law of learning is that attention is necessary for learning.

Another reason you might find something boring is that you have no experience with it in the past. Things we know something about generally spark interest because we can tie the new experience to something known through a process of elaboration. When you know very little, or nothing, about something, it becomes harder to make these connections and as a result they seem boring. In these cases, it might be necessary to use effortful processes of attention to learn enough about the material for it to become interesting. Once it becomes interesting, the effort needed to maintain interest decreases. Think of any sport or activity you enjoy doing. If you start to explain it to someone who knows nothing about it, what is their response? Note that their level of interest will correspond directly to their past experiences. If you are explaining cliff diving and they know nothing about it, but they do know what it would mean to jump a long distance into water, it may be fascinating. If you describe the complicated game of cricket (a distant relative of baseball) and the person to whom you are talking has no idea what baseball is—much less cricket—it is likely to be a very short, and boring (for them), conversation. The trick in learning in college when you don't know enough about the information is to talk to the instructor or read the first blocks of material and force yourself to pay attention through that effortful process. Don't think about the effort, but rather learning enough to see if you can find areas of interest within the topic.

Daydreaming and Attention

Some teachers believe that daydreaming students are just "slackers" who are not interested in learning. To those teachers, attention is totally the responsibility of the student, regardless of their teaching actions. Studies on the brain and learning paint a different picture. The tendency to daydream is a normal brain activity. Essentially everyone finds it difficult to stay focused for more than a few minutes on routine tasks, even if the task somehow captures attention (Smallwood & Schooler, 2006). When attention wanes, so does learning; because of this, those who figure out techniques to improve their ability to pay attention are often the most successful students. We will discuss ways to improve paying attention later in this chapter.

Recent research shows that at times mind wandering can be positive, as it allows us to work through some important thinking. Our brains process information to reach goals, with some of those goals being immediate, whereas others are distant. Somehow, we have evolved a way to switch between handling the here and now and contemplating long-term objectives. It may be no coincidence that most of the thoughts that people have during mind wandering have to do with the future. Even more telling is the discovery that "zoning out" may be the most fruitful type of mind wandering. When we are no longer even aware that our minds are wandering, we may be able to think most deeply about the big picture. So daydreaming isn't bad; in fact, it is important. However, developing the ability to recognize that you are drifting off at a time when you really need to pay attention—in class, for example—is vital to your academic success.

The Impact of Multitasking and Task Shifting on Learning

As humans, it is critical that we be able to do more than one thing at a time. We must be able to watch for traffic and decide when to cross the street, all while walking. We carry on conversations and listen to music while driving, and we can even think about what to have for dinner while riding a bicycle home. We multitask throughout the day. That said, as soon as the demands on our brains exceed a given amount of information, we must transition from multitasking to task shifting. This is typically done without any awareness of it happening. That is the power as well as the trap of the brain, both of which get us into trouble. In addition, there are times during which we have several projects occurring simultaneously. Managing these multiple tasks is vital to keeping the overall project rolling, but this is really neither multitasking nor task shifting. Understanding when it is possible to multitask, the benefits and dangers of task shifting, and the critical elements of managing multiple tasks are critical skills in learning that few give the careful consideration they deserve.

Multitasking and Attention

Being a multitasker is seen by many as a sign of intelligence, kind of like a superhero of brain power. Job advertisements often list the ability to multitask as a critical requirement of the position. The problem is that multitasking is much more complex than most people realize. In cases in which the brain needs to process information, such as reading, listening in class, or being part of a discussion, it is not possible to attend to two tasks at the same time (Foerde, Knowlton, & Poldrack, 2006). In fact, multitasking in these situations violates everything scientists know about how memory works. Imaging studies have indicated that memory tasks and distraction stimuli (reading, listening, etc.) engage different parts of the brain and that these regions compete with each other when we try to multitask, causing both tasks to be disrupted (Foerde et al., 2006). Our brain works hard to fool us into thinking it can process information from more than one source at a time. It can't. When trying to do two cognitively demanding things at once, the brain temporarily shuts down one task while trying to do the other (Dux, Ivanoff, Asplund & Marois, 2006). For example, when you are texting in class you temporarily stop listening to the instructor. If you try to do your homework while texting, watching TV, and talking on the phone, you will find it takes much longer to finish your work and you will likely make many more errors. Psychologist Russell Poldrack warned, "We have to be aware that there is a cost to the way that our society is changing, that humans are not built to multitask. We're really built to focus" (as cited in Rosen, 2008, para. 9). Centuries ago when asked about his particular genius, Isaac Newton responded that any discoveries "owed more to patient attention than to any other talent" (as cited in Rosen, 2008, para. 13).

It is possible to multitask in some situations, but generally not in ways that are conducive to learning new material. Just about any new task in which you engage takes a fair amount of concentration at first. This is called controlled or effortful processing. Some things, if practiced extensively, can become easier and easier to the point that it takes almost no thinking to complete the task. Skiing is a good example of this. When you first start to ski, it is very difficult and demands a great deal of attention. After many hours of practice, you can glide down the slopes with very little effort. When a task becomes very easy to do, it is referred to as automatic processing. We can multitask two automatic processing tasks, such as walking (task 1) and humming a familiar song (task 2). At times, we can even multitask one automatic task and one controlled task, such as driving (automatic) and talking to a friend trying to solve a problem (controlled).

As great as the human brain is, it is next to impossible to pay attention to two controlled things at the same time, such as listening to a lecture of material you do not know well and texting a friend. When your brain does try to work on two controlled processes at the same time, it must stop attention on the first task in order to start attention on the second task. As mentioned before, this is called task shifting. The bottom line is neuroscience evidence has shown constant, intentional self-distraction could well be a profound detriment to individual and cultural well-being (Rosen, 2008).

Managing Multiple Tasks

Although we can't multitask cognitively demanding tasks, what we do much more now than in the past is manage multiple tasks. The two concepts are different. Managing multiple tasks is a skill that must be developed and, once developed, is very valuable. Managing multiple tasks involves appropriately shifting attention, prioritizing resources, and finishing tasks. In fact, many jobs demand successful task managers who can focus their attention on the most important task of the moment and then adapt to changes in task priority as they occur. Think of the emergency room in any big city hospital (Oberlander, Oswald, Hambrick, & Jones, 2007).

Clearly, the ability to handle tasks quickly is an important skill, and many students are good at this. However, even this form of task management has its drawbacks. Studies by Berman, Jonides, and Kaplan (2008) show that even though people feel entertained, even relaxed, when they are managing many tasks, they're actually fatiguing their brains. The drawback to brain fatigue is that our brains need to engage in direct attention to be in a learning mode. When the brain is fatigued, it is much more difficult to focus. Berman and colleagues (2008) also found that irritability in people is often caused by brain fatigue.

Task Shifting

When individuals think of multitasking, they are typically really engaged in a process called task shifting. Task shifting entails jumping quickly between two or more tasks—typically, because at least one of the tasks is controlled to the point that specific cognitive energy is needed. A good example of task shifting is writing a term paper, texting a friend, and watching a television program. All three of these tasks are controlled processes in that they take enough cognitive effort so that when one of the tasks is selected for attention, the other two are "shut down." When you do this your brain will even trick you into thinking that this process is effective. The problem is that many studies have shown that this process is almost always less effective than doing one task at a time. In addition, research shows that task shifting gets more and more inefficient and difficult as we age (Jolly et al., 2016). When you focus on your research paper and take breaks to watch television and text your friends, the paper will be of higher quality and finished much more quickly than if you text friends and have the television on while writing your paper. Even in situations of listening to music and studying at the same time, researchers have found these tasks compete and reduce performance (Christopher & Shelton, 2017). You should listen to music or have the television on while studying only if you need some kind of background sound to keep your brain from being drawn to other sounds in your area. However, for this to work, researchers have found that you must either choose music that is so familiar that it is processed automatically or be sure to cognitively keep the music or television channel in the unattended-to mode—that is, you must ignore the second stimulus. If you are successful, you won't even notice right away if the music happens to stop.

Ways to Improve Your Ability to Pay Attention

Most college professors would agree that the four components of a successful learner are effort, intelligence, background knowledge about the subject to be learned, and the ability to pay attention. They would also likely agree that of these four components, paying attention is the most difficult for today's students. This, however, is likely not the fault of the students. The human brain is wired by every experience it has. If you were born after 1995 you have lived in a media-based culture where information is distributed in very short bits and bytes. This has caused your brain to become used to paying attention for shorter periods of time. Unfortunately, college learning requires a longer attention span. In the next several sections you will find ways to improve your ability to pay attention.

Sleep Improves Attention

Paying attention when you are well rested and interested in the topic is still a challenge given the brain's natural tendency to daydream. Paying attention when you are tired (and sleep deprived) is more than a challenge; it is extremely difficult to do. As we discussed in chapter 2, when the brain is tired or exhausted, it shuts down several of the mental processes that are needed for learning. It does this even though you are still awake. In addition, when you do not get enough sleep, the part of your brain that is most important in paying attention and learning new material, the hippocampus, is unable to ready itself for a new day of learning. This process of clearing away the previous day's unwanted information and passing the important information to the neocortex for memory processing requires a full night's rest (7.5–9 hours). To be ready to pay attention, you must find a way to get enough sleep; otherwise, you are making new learning difficult.

Exercise Improves Attention

As discussed in chapter 3, research clearly shows that people who engage in regular aerobic exercise get a significant boost in their ability to pay attention. This is because the neurochemicals norepinephrine, dopamine, and serotonin are released in the brain in larger amounts when you exercise, and these neurochemicals, especially norepinephrine, enhance your ability to pay attention, focus, concentrate, and maintain motivation to learn (Ratey, 2013). In addition, exercise makes the body healthy and promotes good sleep, which are both important in enhancing your ability to pay attention. Researchers have found that aerobic exercise even boosts the cognitive functioning of children with attention-deficit/hyperactivity disorder (Huang et al., 2014). Doing aerobic exercise (which is always the gold standard) or any exercise four to five days a week is one of the best ways to help improve your ability to pay attention and improve learning.

Be Wary of Easy Ways of Increasing Attention

The Internet is full of suggestions on how to increase your attention span and improve your concentration. However, many of these suggestions are not rooted in any kind of science at all. A 2010 evaluation of purported ways to maintain or improve cognitive function, including attention, conducted for the National Institutes of Health, found many of the claims to be unsupported (Begley, 2011). For example, Vitamins B6, B12, and E; beta carotene; folic acid; and the trendy antioxidants called flavonoids were found to have no value in boosting attention or cognitive functioning. Also, claims that alcohol, omega-3s (the fatty acids in fish), or a large social network improve brain function were found to be weak (Begley, 2011).

There is some solid scientific research, however, on enhancing attention. Meditation has been shown to increase the thickness of brain regions that control attention and process sensory signals from the outside world (Jha, 2011). Meditation has shown success in enhancing mental agility and attention by changing brain structure and function so that brain processes are more efficient, a quality that is associated with higher intelligence (Jha, 2011). These findings came from people who had meditated on a regular basis for 6 months. It is also important to note studies from other areas in the health sciences have demonstrated positive health benefits from meditation such as lowered stress levels (Nidich et al., 2009). In addition, the practice of *mindfulness*, which is defined as a mental state achieved by focusing one's awareness on the present moment, while calmly acknowledging and accepting one's feelings, thoughts, and bodily sensations, also has been found to improve attention (Tang et al., 2010). Mindfulness that requires training has been shown to improve one's ability to pay attention more than current traditional kinds of training. Mindfulness also causes changes in underlying brain activities in areas related to cognition and attention. Tang and his collaborators found that five 20-minute training periods were enough to see improved attention. Many colleges today offer students opportunities for mindfulness training.

Strategies for Enhancing Attention

There are a variety of ways to improve your attention span. Some require little effort and are easy to implement. The suggestions that follow are designed to help you with improving your attention span, but they may take a bit of work to be maximally effective:

1. *Write yourself a message.* It may sound silly to write out a message for yourself, but it works. Writing yourself a note that you can see all the time—for example, on the cover of your notebook or textbook—reminds you to stay on task or pay attention in class.
2. *Fix your environment.* If you need to pay attention, eliminate distractions. Go to the library or study room or find an empty classroom. Turn off your phone (it will be okay, really). In a classroom if possible, sit by students that pay attention and avoid those who are chatty.
3. *Record lectures.* If you record the lecture, or if it is being recorded on a recording tool such as Tegrity, you can stop and start the lecture, making paying attention something you can control.
4. *Focus on the bigger goal.* We went to college and we know classes can sometimes be boring or seem irrelevant. Keep your eye on the bigger goals of graduation and developing your full potential as a way to force yourself to pay attention.

Divide and Conquer

In the end, the best ways to improve your attention are sleep, exercise, meditation, and forcing yourself to pay attention. Attention requires effort and a desire to want to stay focused. In addition, it is often easier to focus and stay attending to a task if you have a goal in mind.

For example, if the task is large (e.g., reading an 80-page chapter), it is easier to stay focused if you divide the task up into manageable parts—say, 20 pages at a time—and then allow yourself a break. It is easy to get overwhelmed by the amount of work that can be required in college, and as a result, you might be distracted by the size of the task, asking yourself, "How am I ever going to get this done?" Focusing on what is doable will help keep you on task and reduce your sense of being overwhelmed.

Athletics and Attention

If you are going to perform your best, it is vital in any sport or activity to "keep your head in the game." In some sports, a single lapse in attention for even a second can result in a loss. Overall, the ability to pay attention to what is unfolding on the court, field, or ice, regardless of other things that might be going on, is often a key to victory. For example, in football it takes focused and effortful attention to not lose your concentration despite an official making a bad call, the opposing team giving you a hard time, weather, poor field conditions, or hostile crowds. This focused attention can be learned and is often something successful athletes are very good at (Murray, 2013). There are also internal distractions, which typically involve some form of negative self-talk, dwelling on a previous mistake, or even overthinking the mechanics of executing or performing. These can also result in losing attention and lead to poor play (Murray 2013).

To be successful athletes must learn how to focus their attention and control their thoughts. It's about being totally in the here-and-now. Peak performance occurs when athletes can focus on the cues in their environment and understand them in a way that allows the athlete to execute the best action within their ability (Nideffer, 1993). Most sports require being able to shift between different types of concentration. The following are types of concentration that are important in sports (Zeplin et al., 2014).

- *External, broad.* This type of concentration involves assessing the environment to explore things like what kind of defense an opponent in basketball is using or how a hole is laid out in golf.

- *Internal, broad.* This type of concentration assists in analyzing the current situation and developing a game plan, such as shifting to a different way of challenging an opponent in soccer.
- *Internal, narrow.* This type of concentration refers to mentally rehearsing a specific shot or movement involved with the task at hand, such as making a free throw in basketball or throwing a curve in baseball or softball.
- *External, narrow.* This type of concentration involves a response while engaged in the sport—taking in what is happening in the environment and reacting instantly without having to think, such as returning a serve in tennis.

One very useful approach to increasing attention and concentration is using preperformance routines. Such routines are commonplace among successful athletes and run the gamut from very subtle to very elaborate—and sometimes quite peculiar. One thing they have in common is that accomplished athletes use them consistently, regardless of whether things are going well or not. A good example is the preshot routine you see every professional golfer go through before every shot. Performance routines work for a number of reasons, including helping athletes block out irrelevant internal and external distractions by giving them something to focus on and enhancing relaxation by providing a sense of familiarity that helps remind athletes this is just another shot, serve, race, or kick. These routines provide athletes with a consistent approach to their sport which, in turn, helps maximize their potential for consistent performance (Bull, Albinson, & Shambrook, 1996).

Many athletes also find the use of attentional cues and triggers to be effective tools in improving their ability to concentrate. Task-related cues help them center their attention on the most appropriate focus within the task at hand (e.g., keep weight/hands back). Cues can also help with more effective aspects of performance (e.g., relax). Usually no more than one or two cues should be used, and their purpose should generally be helping athletes to be focused in the present moment, ready to instinctually react (Bull et al., 1996). Improving your ability to stay focused and pay attention in competitive situations is a big step toward improving your athletic performance. Finding cues and triggers and then practicing routines over and over also allows those actions to become automatic, requiring very little cognitive effort. This allows for multitasking and also the ability to think about more complex aspects of the game. Most importantly, automatic routines allow players to get into the flow and to perform well even when pressure is high.

A Final Thought

The famous biologist and expert on learning James Zull (2002) writes,

> Paying attention does not mean unrelenting attention on one focal point. . . . The brain is more likely to notice details when it scans than when it focuses. . . . It seems, then, that instead of asking people to pay attention, we might ask them to look at things from many different angles. Instead of sitting still, we might ask them to move around so they can see details. (pp. 142–143)

Chapter Summary

It would be wonderful if you just happened to be really interested in everything you are required to learn. If you had only interesting classes with interesting teachers, paying attention would be very easy to do. However, school is at times challenging, difficult, and not all that interesting. Because you learn only what you pay attention to, the information from this chapter is provided to help you improve your ability to pay attention. As noted at the beginning of the chapter, paying attention is not always an easy thing to do. It requires preparing yourself to learn with the proper sleep, diet, and exercise. It requires recognizing when you are daydreaming and bringing your attention back to the task at hand, and it requires ramping up your attention when the learning becomes more challenging. If you follow the suggestions in this chapter, you should be able to improve your ability to pay attention. Following are the key ideas from this chapter:

1. Attention is absolutely necessary for learning.
2. A student's attention span is formed by all of the experiences they had growing up. If you were born after 1995 you grew up in a

media-based culture where information was distributed in short bits and bytes that have likely resulted in you developing a short attention span.

3. Your brain has limitations in terms of how many things can be attended to at the same time.

4. Task shifting leads to extended time to complete a task and increased errors.

5. Everyone daydreams. It is a natural part of the brain's planning and problem-solving process. As you become aware of daydreaming, note if it has added any insights and turn yourself back to the task in hand.

6. Getting enough sleep is crucial to being able to pay attention in class.

7. Aerobic exercise improves attention.

8. Meditation and mindfulness training lead to improved attention.

Critical Thinking and Discussion Questions

1. Attention itself is something that people rarely think about. That said, it is perhaps one of the most important aspects of learning. The next time you read, pay particular attention to the concept of attention while you read a few pages. Does this give you any clues as to how well you attend while you read? What might you do to better focus your attention while reading?

2. List the four different types of attention noted in this chapter. Give an example that you have experienced for each type.

3. List an academic topic or concept that you must learn about this semester that seems boring to you. For whatever you listed, why do you think it is boring? That is, what is the reason for not finding the topic interesting? This can't be simply "I'm just not interested in this." Rather, it is a deeper dive into why you are not interested. What might you do to attempt making this seem more interesting to you?

4. Explain the difference, in your own words, between multitasking, task shifting, and managing multiple tasks. Give one example of

something you can multitask and one example of when you have noticed yourself task shifting. Explain a time when you were task shifting and suddenly realized that you were very engaged in one of the tasks and forgot to "shift" back to the other.

5. In sports we often say a player "lost focus." This means that he or she lost attention. Explain a time when you saw a player who you believe lost attention during an event or game, or watch a sporting event and look for this brief loss of attention. In this situation, what do you think caused the attentional difficulty? Is there anything you noted that might help the player maintain attention in the future?

References

Bach, R. (1977). *Illusions: The adventures of a reluctant messiah*. New York, NY: Dell.

Begley, S. (2011, January 3). Can you build a better brain? *Newsweek*. Retrieved from http://www.newsweek.com/can-you-build-better-brain-66769

Berman, M., Jonides, J., & Kaplan, S. (2008, December). The cognitive benefits of interacting with nature. *Psychological Science, 19*, 1207–1212.

Bruya, B. (2010). *Effortless attention: A new perspective on the cognitive science of attention and action*. Cambridge, MA: MIT Press.

Bull, S. J., Albinson, J. G., & Shambrook, C. J. (1996). *The mental game plan*. Cheltenham, UK: Sports Dynamics.

Carp, J., Fitzgerald, K. D., Taylor, S. F., & Weissman, D. H. (2012). Removing the effect of response time on brain activity reveals developmental differences in conflict processing in the posterior medial prefrontal cortex. *NeuroImage, 59*, 853–860.

Christopher, E. A., & Shelton, J. T. (2017). Individual differences in working memory predict the effect of music on student performance. *Journal of Applied Research in Memory and Cognition, 6*(2), 167–173.

Csikszentmihalyi, M. (2014). *Flow and the foundation of positive psychology*. New York, NY: Springer.

Dawson, M., & Medler, D. (2009). Sustained attention. *Dictionary of cognitive science*. Retrieved from http://www.bcp.psych.ualberta.ca/~mike/Pearl_Street/Dictionary/contents/S/sustained_attention.html

Dux, P. E., Ivanoff, J., Asplund, C. L., & Marois, R. (2006). Isolation of a central bottleneck of information processing with time-resolved FMRI. *Neuron. 52*(6), 1109–1120.

Foerde, K., Knowlton, B., & Poldrack, R. (2006). Modulation of competing memory systems by distraction. *Proceedings of the National Academy of Sciences of the United States of America, 103*(31), 11778–11783.

Huang, C.-J., Huant, C.-W., Tsai, Y.-J., Tsai, C.-L., Chang, Y.-K., & Hung, T.-M. (2014). A preliminary examination of aerobic exercise effects on resting EEG in children with ADHD. *Journal of Attention Disorders, 21*(11), 898–903.

Jha, A. (2011). Meditation improves brain anatomy and function. *Psychiatry Research Neuroimaging, 191*(1), 1–86.

Jolly, T. A. D., Cooper, P. S., Rennie, J. L., Levi, C. R., Lenroot, R., Parsons, M. W., . . . Karayanidis, F. (2016). Age-related decline in task switching is linked to both global and track-specific changes in white matter microstructure. *Human Brain Mapping, 38*, 1588–1603.

McSpadden, K. (2015, May 14). You now have a shorter attention span than a goldfish. *Time.* Retrieved from http://time.com/3858309/attention-spans-goldfish/

Montagne, R. (2011, January. 5). The incredible shrinking sound bite. Retrieved from https://www.npr.org/2011/01/05/132671410/Congressional-Sound-Bites

Murray, J. (2013, April 21). Concentration is crucial in football [Web log post]. Retrieved from http://www.johnfmurray.com/sport/football/concentration-is-crucial-in-football/

Nideffer, R. M. (1993). Concentration and attention control training. In J. M. Williams (Ed.), *Applied sport psychology: Personal growth to peak performance* (pp. 257–269). Mountain View, CA: Mayfield.

Nidich, S. I., Fields, J. Z., Rainforth, M. V., Pomerantz, R., Cella, D., Kristeller, J., . . . Schneider, R. H. (2009). A randomized controlled trial of the effects of transcendental meditation on quality of life in older breast cancer patients. *Integrative Cancer Therapies, 8*(3), 228–234.

Oberlander, E., Oswald, F., Hambrick, D., & Jones, L. (2007). *Individual difference variables as predictors of error during multitasking.* Millington, TN: Navy Personnel Research, Studies, and Technology Division.

Osman, M. (2004). An evaluation of dual-process theories of reasoning. *Psychonomic Bulletin & Review, 11*(6), 988–1010.

Ratey, J. (2013). *Spark: The revolutionary new science of exercise and the brain.* New York, NY: Little Brown.

Rosen, C. (2008). The myth of multitasking. *The New Atlantis.* Retrieved from http://www.thenewatlantis.com/publications/the-myth-of-multitasking

Smallwood, J., & Schooler, J. (2006). The restless mind. *Psychological Bulletin, 132*(6), 946–958.

Swing, E., Gentile, D., Anderson, C., & Walsh, D. (2010, July 5). Television and video game exposure and the development of attention problems. *Pediatrics.* Retrieved from http://pediatrics.aappublications.org/content/early/2010/07/05/peds.2009-1508

Tang, Y. Y., Lu, Q., Geng, X., Stein, E. A., Yang, Y., & Posner, M. I. (2010). Short term meditation induces white matter changes in anterior cingulate. *Proceedings of the National Academy of Sciences of the United States of America, 107*(35), 15649–15642.

Zeplin, S., Galli, N., Visek, A. J., Durham, W., & Staples, J. (2014, May). Concentration and attention in sport [Factsheet]. *Exercise and Sport Psychology.* Retrieved from http://www.apadivisions.org/division-47/publications/sportpsych-works/concentration-and-attention.pdf

Zull, J. (2002). *The art of changing the brain.* Sterling, VA: Stylus.

9

A MESSAGE FROM
THE AUTHORS

One of the great benefits a college student today has over previous generations of college students has come about through the development of neuroimaging tools that allow, for the first time in human history, scientists to look inside the human brain and see how it operates. As a result, today's students have accurate, scientifically proven information about how the brain learns and remembers information and skills, whereas those who came before just had to guess. What we have tried to do in this book is guide you through the new evidence and techniques in a way that made it easy for you to implement them into your own life. The information in this book is not our opinion but rather scientific evidence about what actions work and should be integrated into your daily life as a student and lifelong learner. The basic finding that we have reinforced throughout this book is that the *one who does the work does the learning*. There is, unfortunately, no magic pill that you can take to make learning easy—at least not yet. The brain can hang on to new learning it encounters every day only by hard work and continued practice. We believe that by implementing the information discussed in this book you will be maximizing your brain's ability to learn and that is all anyone can ask of you.

Employment and College Success

In 1973 only 28% of all jobs in the United States required postsecondary education. A 2015 Georgetown study shows that since 2008 11.6 million new jobs have been created in the United States. Of these, 11.5 million went to people with some college course work. The same study indicated that there were 2.9 million "good" jobs" created, meaning the jobs pay $53,000 or more and tend to be full time with lucrative benefits such as 401(k) contributions, training, and health care. Of these 2.9 million good jobs, less than 100,000 were filled by people with less than a bachelor's degree (Carnevale, Rose, & Cheah, 2011). A college degree and a set of learning skills that will allow you to compete in the world marketplace has become essential. Add to this change in employment expectations the extraordinary pace of change and growth of knowledge in the world in which you live and will continue to live for the next 80 years or so and you have a clear picture of why you need to learn in harmony with your brain.

The Pace of Change in Technology

Nowhere has the pace of change been greater than in the technology segment of our society. Just one example is if we compare the 1971 Intel computer processing chip (4004) to the 2016 chip. Today's Intel chip has 3,500 times more processing power/performance, is 90,000 times more energy efficient, and is 60,000 times lower in cost (Friedman, 2016). According to the CEO of Intel, if we compare this pace of change to what would have had to happen to a Volkswagen Beetle made in 1971, today's Beetle would go 300,000 mph, get two million miles per gallon, and cost four cents (Friedman, 2016).

Another example is in the production of parts for manufacturing. Luana Lorio, director of the GE three-dimensional manufacturing unit, said in an interview that

> in the past, creating a new part could take two years from when you first had the idea—now using a 3D printer you can design it, send it to the printer, and the part appears before your very eyes—you can immediately test it as many times as you want in one day, making changes and getting a new printed part and within a week you have the new part. (Friedman, 2016, chapter 3)

The pace of change in technology is extraordinary and will present a continuing challenge to all learners to try to keep pace.

Becoming a Lifelong Learner

Most of you reading this book are part of the first generation for whom having a college degree will be only the starting point of your life as a learner. Using your college experience to not only earn a degree but also become a successful lifelong learner, capable of updating your skills and knowledge as you need to, will be a significant determiner of your long-term success. A major goal of higher education is to create lifelong learners—intentional, independent, self-directed learners who can acquire, retain, and retrieve new knowledge on their own (National Leadership Council for Liberal Education and American Promise, 2007; Wirth, 2008). One of the hopes we had in writing this book was to help you in some small way prepare for this extraordinary future.

Learning Takes a Lot of Time and Practice

One of the most important messages in this book is that learning anything new takes more time, practice, and skill than most people realize. The human brain strengthens memories each time they are recalled. The more often something gets practiced, the stronger the memory becomes. The important point is that there is really no substitute for practice over time if you want to really learn something new. The more ways you use the information (elaboration, discussed in chapter 6) and the more times you recall the information (long-term potentiation, discussed in chapter 1), the greater the likelihood that you will be able to recall the information or skill when you need it. Accepting this fact about the work needed to establish long-term memories and acting accordingly can lead to long-term learning success.

Preparing to Learn

The human brain is an amazing, complex, and beautiful organ, but it needs to be cared for with sleep, hydration, nutrition, and exercise for it to operate at its best. When you prepare your brain to learn by getting 7.5 to 9 hours of sleep each night, engage in aerobic exercise four to five times a week, and make certain that your brain is hydrated and has the energy from food that it needs to operate at its best, then you are truly prepared to learn. This is a whole new level of responsibility that you must be willing to accept. Prior generations didn't know how important these four actions were to the brain's ability to learn, so for them there was a very regimented prescription for learning—students simply repeated back the information teachers told them. With new discoveries come new opportunities and new responsibilities. Preparing your brain for learning is crucial to your college and lifelong success.

Being a Self-Regulated Learner

Learning is not something that happens to you. As we have said many times in this book, it is the one who does the work who does the learning. You cannot look to your instructor and say, "Please teach me." Yes, instructors have a great responsibility in facilitating your education, but only your intentional effort to learn will result in academic success. Numerous studies show that many college students think their failure is the result of poor teaching, too difficult course work, or irrelevant content (Elliott, 2010). Many actually express that they have no interest in learning at all. They are in college because they see it as the only path to a job (Pryor, Hurtado, DeAngelo, Palucki Blake, & Tran, 2011). We understand that some of these concerns are valid, but we also suggest that if you are to be academically successful, you must not use these concerns as excuses to not do well.

We hope that you will use the information in this book to become a more self-regulated learner. A self-regulated learner is one who, first, has a goal for every learning experience (Nilson, 2013). What do you want to get out of this learning experience? Do you want to learn for practical reasons like earning an A in this class, or for more personal reasons like learning more about this subject so you can use it to develop your readiness for your adult life career? The second step is having a plan as to how to reach your learning goal. It might include how you plan to stay awake and pay attention, how you plan to take notes or ask questions, where you will write down assignments and due dates, or how to read the chapter, so you understand and can recall the essential information. This step also includes how you plan to stay on task to get outside work completed, when you will take breaks so your brain can rest, and when you will sleep so you can make memories and be ready to learn the next day.

The third step is recognizing whether or not your learning approaches and strategies are working effectively and efficiently for you. Are you, in fact, understanding the material, are your answers to assigned questions well thought out, or is your written assignment well-constructed and organized (Nilson, 2013)? Being self-regulated means using the information in this book to make yourself a more effective and efficient learner who doesn't leave things to chance, saying, "I hope I get a good grade." In the end your success can be greatly enhanced by being a self-regulated learner who is truly open to learning in harmony with your brain.

Money Matters

College graduates have known for decades that their degrees almost always mean more money and greater opportunity. Recent studies show that the income gap between those with only a high school diploma and college graduates is widening. The difference in income level for those who complete college and can continue to update their skills and knowledge to remain productive in their careers and professions is two to four times higher over a lifetime than those who earn only a high school diploma (Carnevale, Rose, & Cheah, 2011). Accepting the responsibility to maximize your brain's learning abilities so you can compete in the job market will play a significant role in what happens to you over the course of your lifetime.

What Is Not in This Book

In writing this book, we made a conscious decision not to include information about study strategies or study skills. Study skills and strategies are important, but there is an endless number of fine websites and books that can suggest strategies you will find helpful in aiding your learning and studying activities. One excellent site is www.academictips.org. You will also find excellent help on your own campus, as every college now has student academic support centers where help in choosing the right study or learning strategy is just a phone call or an e-mail away.

We also decided to not fully address the social and emotional issues that play a significant role in helping or interfering with learning for similar reasons. Social and emotional factors have a profound impact on the learning process. Note, for example, the role stress plays in memory, as discussed in chapter 6. We know that your college experience is also about learning how to deal with oneself, others, and relationships in an effective manner; developing affective tools, like sympathy and empathy for others; and maintaining positive relationships. We believe these issues are very important, and we know that much has already been written about their role in enhancing or deterring effective learning. For example, using study groups or peer group learning, finding a mentor, or being involved in campus organizations where you can learn leadership skills or enhance your cooperation skills are all important to your overall learning experience. There is significant evidence that collaborative learning activities often lead to enhanced understanding and exposure to new insights and views that would be lost if one worked solely alone. We also recognize that learning to develop a set of values and ideas that will guide your life is also part of a complete college experience. In the appendix we provide a few excellent resources that might help you in developing these social and emotional skills. Just as all campuses have resources for helping with study skills and strategies, all colleges also have numerous organizations and support systems in place to help students develop their social and emotional skill set, and we encourage you to use them. Keep in mind that using these services does not represent any weakness on your part but rather an opportunity for you to be successful. Professionals in counseling programs, student success centers, and other resource offices are there to assist. They are often some of the most helpful and friendly people on campus.

A Final Thought—Find Balance in Your Life

Your life in college and after will be filled with challenges that will require a brain that is optimized for learning, but your brain is not the only thing that will matter. To find success in college and in life, you need to find a balance between the demands of academic life and the joys, pleasures, and people that make your life meaningful. What we wish for you is that you find balance in all aspects of your life— your sleep, exercise, diet, social life, emotional health, and academic endeavors—and that you remember to learn in harmony with your brain.

Critical Thinking and Discussion Questions

1. Summarize the resources that exist at your campus for academic support and social/emotional support. Once you have finished your summary, ask three friends to tell you quickly what support exists on campus in these areas. Did you know about these support areas previously; did your friends? What did you find in doing this exercise that you expected and what surprised you?

2. What types of skills or knowledge do you think you will need to do the kind of work you hope to do after graduation? How can you continue to develop those skills? That is, what can you do to ensure you get the educational experience you hope to receive while in college?

References

Carnevale, A., Rose, S., & Cheah, B. (2011). *The college payoff.* Washington DC: Georgetown University Center on Education and the Workforce. Retrieved from https://www2.ed.gov/policy/highered/reg/hearulemaking/2011/collegepayoff.pdf

Elliott, D. (2010, August 1). How to teach the trophy generation. *Chronicle of Higher Education.* Retrieved from http://chronicle.com/article/How-to-teach-the-trophy-generation/123723/?sid=pm&utm_medium=en

Friedman, T. (2016). *Thank you for being late: An optimist's guide to thriving in the age of accelerations* [Kindle Fire Version]. New York, NY: Picador Press.

National Leadership Council for Liberal Education and American Promise. (2007). College Learning for the New Global Century. Retrieved June 3, 2018 from https://www.aacu.org/sites/default/files/files/LEAP/GlobalCentury_final.pdf

Nilson, L. (2013). *Creating self-regulated learners: Strategies to strengthen students' self-awareness and learning skills.* Sterling, VA: Stylus.

Pryor, J. H., Hurtado, S., DeAngelo, L., Palucki Blake, L., & Tran, S. (2011). *The American freshman: National norms fall 2010.* Los Angeles, CA: Higher Education Research Institute, University of California, Los Angeles.

Wirth, K. (2008). *Learning about thinking and thinking about learning: Metacognitive knowledge and skills for intentional learners.* Retrieved from https://serc.carleton.edu/NAGTWorkshops/metacognition/workshop08/participants/wirth.html

APPENDIX

Education Continues to Change

About 20 years ago higher education began a dramatic shift from a focus on teaching to a focus on learning. That shift is still happening today and will continue to happen for years to come. The difference sounds subtle but has enormous implications on what you, as a student, will experience in the classroom. A teaching-oriented classroom has a focus on covering content and the teaching strategy most often encountered is the lecture, with little contribution by the student in a given class period. A learning-oriented classroom has a focus on determining the extent to which students have learned. Learning-centered classrooms require students to produce responses, talk to one another, and engage in behaviors that allow a faculty member to identify whether the learning goals have been met. This means you will be engaged much more in a learning-oriented classroom than you will in a teaching-oriented classroom. The good news is that the learning-oriented approach is much more aligned with how the brain best learns. You have seen these strategies noted throughout this book in areas such as multisensory learning, pattern recognition, and practicing at recall.

Don't Wait to Seek Help

One of the most visible signs that you are an intelligent, interested, and committed student is that you seek help when you need it. Research by

Carnegie Mellon University (www.cmu.edu/teaching/solveproblem/strat-dontseekhelp/index.html) and others show the students who most need assistance with their academic or personal issues are the ones who are least likely to seek it out. Attending office hours to get help in a class, signing up for tutoring when the course is difficult for you, going to the writing center for help on a paper, speaking to your adviser when you need assistance about what program/career to pursue, or going to a personal counselor when life gets a bit overwhelming are all signs that you care about your own well-being and are smart enough to seek help when you need it. No one gets through the rigors of college without needing help at one time or another. The smartest thing you can do to be a successful college student is to get help when you need it.

Cooperation and Teamwork

You will be required to work in groups or as a team member many times in your college courses. In some cases, faculty members will give you tips regarding effective teamwork, and in other cases you will be taught how to work well in teams as part of the group assignment. That said, in many cases your teachers will focus on the content and expected outcomes of the group project, but not give you any guidance at all on the process of working in groups or on teams. Given the number of times you will work in teams, and the value of being a good team member when you look for jobs after graduation, it is extremely beneficial to study on your own about what makes an effective team. Becoming knowledgeable about effective teams will often land you in the role of team leader. Learning how to handle team members who are less cooperative or simply don't do their work is a great skill to possess. Having experience in running small teams will certainly be a benefit to you at a later time. Take a bit of time over breaks and read up on effective teamwork; business executives do that all the time. Visit www.imperial.ac.uk/students/success-guide/ug/effective-study/working-with-others/effective-team-work for an example of material that can help you to be a team leader.

Peer Study Groups

Study groups involve two or more students who meet to share information, knowledge, and expertise about a course in which they are all enrolled. Study groups offer students an opportunity to engage in a more in-depth discussion about course material. Students working in small groups typically learn more of what has been taught and retain it longer than when simply hearing the material through a lecture. When working in a study group, it is important to create an agenda or some expectation for the group and then stick to learning. It is fine to take breaks, but when working it is important to focus on the material to be learned. Your time is extremely valuable and if the group is not focused on learning, look for another group. Visit www.montclair.edu/media/ montclairedu/residentialeducation/pdffiles/Study-Group-Tips-and-Advantages-1.pdf to learn more about study groups

Finding a Mentor

A 2014 Gallup and Purdue University study involving 30,000 college graduates found that having a mentor was one of the most important and beneficial things that can happen to students during their college life. Individuals in a wide variety of professional roles have multiple mentors. Mentors are crucial in helping you to make critical decisions in life. Be on the lookout for potential mentors as you move through college and early in your career. The most likely people who will become mentors for you will be your course instructors or academic advisers. These are the people you see on a regular basis and as a result you have the opportunity to build a more personal relationship with them. A great way to get to know instructors or advisers is to attend their office hours when you can speak to them on a one-to-one basis. Another effective way to build a more personal relationship is by staying after class to ask a question, which shows you are interested in learning the course material and gives you a chance to speak to the instructor one-on-one. There is a wide variety of published materials that describe both the value of mentors and how to go about getting them. Go to

www.huffingtonpost.com/her-campus/post_3086_b_1324242.html
to read more about finding a mentor.

Living a Balanced Life

If you are like most college students, you are frequently exhausted. If you feel that college is extremely demanding on your time and that after college you will have more time to sleep and to do hobbies, I am afraid we have some bad news for you. Being busy and exhausted is a way of life. If you do it now, it is likely you will do it later as well. Most individuals don't stop to consider that obligations and opportunities will not decrease when you graduate, start a new job, or have a family. Now is the time to start living a balanced life. There are certainly times when demands will stack up, such as during exam week, but you should not be tired all the time. A well-balanced life is important for your personal effectiveness and peace of mind. There is always someone, or something, you must answer to. There are things we want to do and things we must do. The challenge is to balance what we must do with what we enjoy and want to do. This is not always easy, and it won't get easier later. You will make mistakes at times, but if you engage in some study in this area, you can live a more balanced life. Visit www.essentiallifeskills.net/wellbalancedlife.html for some tips on how to get started living a balanced life.

INDEX

ing?

memories and, 23, 25–26, 45, 102–4, 106, 120
memory traces movement of, 24
new learning and, 103–4
non-REM, 23–24
patterns, 23–25, 27–31, 45
protein and, 102
quality of, 35
REM, 23–24, 26–27, 36–38, 44, 103–4
remembering what is important during, 33
researchers on, 23
spindles, 25, 104
stages of, 27
stress management for, 41
students and, 21–22, 33–35, 45
studying before, 106
transference during, 23
sleep debt
definition of, 34
fixing of, 38–40
naps and, 39
sleep deprivation
causes of, 35–39
learning difficulty of, 26
lower grade point average and, 22
low glucose levels and, 43
memory impairment of, 34–35
of night owls, 29
Sleep Is the New Status Symbol, 21
slow-wave sleep. See deep NREM
Small, Scott, 57
smell, 69–70, 78
smoking, 53
Spark: The Revolutionary New Science of Exercise and the Brain (Ratey), 51–52, 57

Sports Medicine, 44
Squire, L. R., 105
stage n1, as transition to sleep, 27
stage n2, as light sleep, 27
stage n3, as deep sleep, 27
standing desks, 59
Stanford University, 126
Sleep Clinic, 31
stationary bikes, 59–60, 62
storage, 26
stress, 117
students
academic support centers for, 169
daydreaming, 149–50
difficult material and, 15–16
exercise and, 52, 56, 59–61
fixed mindsets and, 131
forgetfulness of, 115–16, 120
honor students and, 3
learning-centered teaching and, 10–11, 173
learning goals and, 130
mastery-oriented, 130
multisensory learning and, 66–69
naps and, 115
neuroimaging tools and, 164
as night owls, 29
reading and, 76
sleep and, 21–22, 33–35, 45
study skills, 168
emotional issues and, 169
student academic support centers for, 169
websites for, 169
successful learner, components of, 153–54
sugar
carbohydrates and, 11